McGraw-Hill Education

500
ACT English and
Reading Questions

to Know by Test Day

Second Edition

Anaxos, Inc.

New York   Chicago   San Francisco   Athens   London   Madrid
Mexico City   Milan   New Delhi   Singapore   Sydney   Toronto

1 2 3 4 5 6 7 8 9   QFR   23 22 21 20 19 18

ISBN   978-1-260-10832-3
MHID   1-260-10832-5

e-ISBN   978-1-260-10833-0
e-MHID   1-260-10833-3

ACT is a registered trademark of ACT, Inc., which was not involved in the production of, and does not endorse, this product.

McGraw-Hill Education products are available at special quantity discounts to use as premiums and sales promotions or for use in corporate training programs. To contact a representative, please visit the Contact Us pages at www.mhprofessional.com.

CONTENTS

INTRODUCTION

Congratulations! You've taken a big step toward ACT success by purchasing *McGraw-Hill Education 500 ACT English and Reading Questions to Know by Test Day*, Second Edition. We are here to help you take the next step and score high on your ACT exam so you can get into the college or university of your choice!

This book gives you 500 ACT-style multiple-choice questions that cover all the most essential reading and writing material. The questions will give you valuable independent practice to supplement your regular textbook and the ground you have already covered in your English and reading class. Each question is clearly explained in the answer key.

The passages presented here cover the same broad categories (prose fiction, humanities, social sciences, and natural sciences) as the ACT. On the ACT, these passages appear in no particular order, and so the passages here are presented in a similar random order.

In addition, this book includes an explanation for writing the ACT essay. First, it takes you step-by-step through the writing process, and then it provides prompts that allow you to practice your writing skills on your own.

This book and the others in the series were written by expert teachers who know the ACT inside and out and can identify crucial information as well as the kinds of questions that are most likely to appear on the exam.

You might be the kind of student who needs to study extra a few weeks before the exam for a final review. Or you might be the kind of student who puts off preparing until the last minute before the exam. No matter what your preparation style, you will benefit from reviewing these 500 questions, which closely parallel the content, format, and degree of difficulty of the reading and English questions on the actual ACT exam. These questions and the explanations in the answer key are the ideal last-minute study tool for those final weeks before the test.

If you practice with all the questions and answers in this book, we are certain you will build the skills and confidence needed to excel on the ACT. Good luck!

—Editors of McGraw-Hill Education

PART 1

Reading

CHAPTER 1

Set 1 Reading Questions

Prose Fiction

"Love of Life" by Jack London

This selection is the end of a story about a man who had starved in the wilderness for several days. Hungry and sick, he crawled to a beach, where he was taken aboard a ship filled with scientists.

He was lost and alone, sick and injured too badly to walk upright. He crawled on. There came frightful days of snow and rain. He did not know when he made camp, when he broke camp. He traveled in the night as much as in the day. He rested wherever he fell and crawled on whenever the dying life in him flickered up and burned less dimly. He did not try. It 5 was the life in him, unwilling to die, that drove him on. He didn't suffer. His nerves had become blunted and numb, while his mind was filled with weird visions and delicious dreams.

There were some members of a scientific expedition on the whaleship *Bedford*. From the deck they saw a strange object on the shore. It was on 10 the beach, moving towards the water. They couldn't tell what it was. Being scientists, they took a boat to see. They saw something alive, but it hardly looked like a man. It was blind, unconscious, and crawled on the beach like a giant worm. Most of its effort to crawl was useless, but it kept trying. It turned and twisted, moving about 20 feet an hour. 15

Three weeks afterwards the man lay in a bunk on the whaleship, and with tears streaming down his wasted cheeks told who he was and what he had undergone. He also babbled words that made no sense: about his mother, of sunny Southern California, and a home among the orange groves and flowers. 20

The days were not many after that when he sat at the table with the scientific men and ship's officers. He was happy over the sight of so much food, watching it anxiously as it went into the mouths of others. With the disappearance of each mouthful, an expression of deep regret came into

his eyes. He was quite sane, yet he hated those men at mealtimes because they ate 25
so much food. He was haunted by a fear that it would not last. He inquired of the
cook, the cabin-boy, the captain concerning the food stores. They reassured him
countless times; but he could not believe them and pried cunningly about the food
storage chest to see with his own eyes.

It was noticed that the man was getting fat. He grew stouter with each day. The 30
scientific men shook their heads and theorized. They limited the man at his meals,
but still his girth increased and his body grew fatter under his shirt.

The sailors grinned. They knew. And when the scientific men followed the
man, they knew, too. They saw him bent over after breakfast, and like a mendicant,
with outstretched palm, stop a sailor. The sailor grinned and passed him a fragment 35
of sea biscuit. He clutched it avariciously, looking at it as a miser looks at gold, and
thrust it inside his shirt. Similar were the donations from other grinning sailors.

The scientific men respected the man's privacy. They left him alone. But they
secretly examined his bunk. It was lined with seamen's crackers; the mattress was
stuffed with crackers; every nook and cranny was filled with crackers. Yet he was 40
sane. He was taking precautions against another possible famine—that was all. He
would recover from it, the scientific men said; and he did, 'ere the *Bedford's* anchor
rumbled down in San Francisco Bay.

1. The point of view from which the passage is told can best be described as
   that of a

   (A) scientist who traveled on the *Bedford* and met the man in the story.
   (B) narrator who is able to see and understand every aspect of the main
       character.
   (C) friend of the man who learned of the man's plight and helped him
       recover.
   (D) narrator who is describing his own experiences and how he was
       affected by them.

2. When the author describes the man by saying that "the dying life in him
   flickered up and burned less dimly," he is comparing the man's life to

   (A) death.
   (B) dimness.
   (C) insanity.
   (D) a candle.

3. It can reasonably be inferred from the second paragraph (lines 9–15) that
   the man

   (A) was trying to get their attention.
   (B) was unhappy to see the scientists.
   (C) looked more like an animal than a human.
   (D) was a dangerous person.

4. Which of the following best describes the man's predicament?
    (A) There wasn't enough food on the ship.
    (B) The scientists aboard the ship were too harsh with him.
    (C) The man needed to recover from a terrible ordeal.
    (D) The man needed transportation to San Francisco.

5. When the author says that the man looked at a piece of sea biscuit "as a miser looks at gold," he means that the man
    (A) thought the sea biscuit was inedible.
    (B) wanted to hoard it.
    (C) wanted nothing to do with it.
    (D) got sick just looking at it.

6. It can reasonably be inferred from the passage that the man stored biscuits in his mattress because
    (A) he wanted to make sure he always had food.
    (B) he knew that biscuits were in short supply and would soon run out.
    (C) he was a thief.
    (D) he was very fond of sea biscuits.

7. In the sixth paragraph (lines 33–37), the author compares the man to a mendicant, which means that he was
    (A) begging.
    (B) crying.
    (C) arguing.
    (D) experimenting.

8. It can reasonably be inferred from the fourth paragraph (lines 21–29) that the man hated the people eating with him because
    (A) he disliked scientists.
    (B) they were unfriendly to him.
    (C) he thought they were taking food that he would need.
    (D) they had few manners.

9. Which of the following statements about the sailors is supported by the passage?
    (A) They thought he might hurt them if they didn't help him.
    (B) They thought he was a curiosity and went along with his requests.
    (C) They wanted the man to gain weight, since he had been starving.
    (D) They hoped that the man would help them when they were in need.

10. The passage discusses everything about the man EXCEPT his
    (A) appearance.
    (B) name.
    (C) past.
    (D) attitude toward food.

11. It can reasonably be inferred that the man could be seen as a symbol of
    (A) greed and unpleasantness.
    (B) humanity's desire to survive.
    (C) the failures of humankind.
    (D) the power of science.

12. According to the passage, what would most likely happen to the man?
    (A) He would lose his obsession with food.
    (B) He would never recover his sanity.
    (C) He would stay convinced that he would starve.
    (D) He would steal more and more.

13. It can reasonably be inferred that the main theme of the passage is that
    (A) scientists are kind people.
    (B) starvation can affect a person's mind.
    (C) sailors are helpful to sick people.
    (D) some people are unable to control their desire for food.

Paired Passages: Social Sciences

Passage 1: The Great Stilt Race

This account of a bizarre event in the late 1800s is true, proving that truth can be stranger than fiction.

One of the most unusual and grueling races ever to be run was the great stilt race that took place in southwestern France in the late 1800s. Walking on stilts requires a good sense of balance and a great deal of practice, but the men who competed in the great stilt race were experts. It may seem that it would be difficult for the organizers of a stilt race to gather enough contestants to compete in such   5
an unusual contest. But this was not the case in the particular area of France where the race took place.

In southwestern France, there is a large, flat section of land known as "Les Landes." The people who live there are shepherds, and in order to keep a close watch over their herds, they have to overcome one formidable obstacle—the   10
undrained lagoons and marshes covering Les Landes, which make normal walking impossible. So that they could navigate these ditches and wet areas, the shepherds of Les Landes took to wearing stilts.

The stilt race was organized because a local newspaper was looking for a way to increase its circulation. When a journalist happened to see two shepherds 15 from Les Landes on stilts heading at top speed down a country road, an idea began to form in his mind. Shortly afterward, the newspaper was offering a prize of $170 and a gold medal to the winner of a race run on stilts. The response from the local people was overwhelming—before long, 75 men had entered the competition. 20

The rules of the race were simple. The contestants were to walk on stilts along a 305-mile-long course across the French countryside. Estimates put the time necessary to complete the trip at eight and a half days. At 9:22 on the morning of May 26, the 75 contestants took off, covering about two yards with each step. Hundreds of spectators lined the road, eyeing the contestants and eagerly placing 25 bets on their favorites.

The course took the men first along paved roads, then over dirt roads farther out in the country, and finally into the hills. All along the route, proprietors of local cafés rushed out with glasses of wine to refresh the parched throats of the competitors. Stopping for just a moment, but without dismounting, a racer 30 would reach down, take the glass, quickly down its contents, and continue on his way.

The biggest problems the racers encountered were fatigue, blisters, and chafed legs. These problems took their toll: about halfway through the race, the field had narrowed to only 32 contestants, a fact that did not surprise the organizers. 35

Finally, on May 30, the first weary and dust-covered competitor dragged himself over the finish line in Bordeaux. He had completed the course in just over 100 hours, averaging about three miles per hour over the entire trip.

Hundreds of fans and a brass band were there to greet the winner. As for the rest of the competitors—well, by the time they got to the finish line, the festivities 40 honoring the winner were well underway. They were certainly welcome to join in, but most of them were too tired.

Passage 2: The Creation of the Tour de France

This passage recounts the early years of the Tour de France, which was rife with claims of cheating.

The Tour de France was the brainchild of journalist Geo Lefevre, who worked for the struggling sports newspaper *L'Auto*. He came up with the idea to boost newspaper sales and took it to the director-editor, Henri Desgrange. Desgrange was a cyclist himself and loved the notion. The final design included a 1,500-mile circuit that looped through France, beginning and ending in the country's capital, 5 Paris. Early in the morning on July 1, 1903, sixty bicyclists eagerly lined up. They were spurred on by the challenge of an unprecedented test of endurance and also by the enticement of the reward: 20,000 francs.

This inaugural race was quite different from the Tour de France 100 years later. There were no Alpine climbs, and it included only six stages. These cyclists, how- 10 ever, raced on unpaved roads without helmets. They also had to endure gruel- ing stages—an average of 250 miles. These long stages meant that the cyclists rode through the night. The rules were different, too. There was no riding in a slipstream or receiving support from cars that followed along. The cyclists were also responsible for their own repairs and rode with spare tires and tubes strapped 15 around their waists.

The first leg of the race was almost 300 miles long and it took the winner, Maurice Garin, 17 hours to complete. Shockingly, he won by a margin of just one minute. Eventually, the field of competitors dropped to just 21, and Garin widened his lead. After 95 hours of riding, Garin won the first Tour de France by 20 a resounding three hours—a lead that has not been matched since.

There are a few things that have not changed about the Tour de France over its long and checkered history. One of them is its fame as a remarkable test of endur- ance for its competitors. Another is its reputation for chicanery. In the very first race, one of the favorites, Hippolyte Aucouturier, dropped out after experiencing 25 stomach cramps, most likely the result of his use of red wine as an early 1900s version of a performance enhancer. Another cyclist, Jean Fischer, was disqualified for having a car pace him. Still another cyclist was removed for riding in a car's slipstream.

The next year, even more controversy beset the race. Fans of a hometown cyclist 30 created a blockade to prevent other cyclists from getting through and even attacked the competitors. Other fans placed tacks and broken glass on the course when their favorite was disqualified. The riders were also unscrupulous. Some of them took rides during the dark and received help from outsiders. Garin appeared to be the winner of the second Tour de France; however, he was stripped of that title after he 35 was accused of illegally obtaining food. Although it continued to be plagued with controversy, the race accomplished its purpose: newspaper sales. *L'Auto* reported a sixfold increase in sales during the Tour de France, and it became an annual event.

Passage 1 Questions

14. The main point of this passage is to
   (A) illustrate the difficulties of walking long distances on stilts.
   (B) recount the story of a strange race with stilts that took place in the late 1800s.
   (C) deliberate why the winner was so much faster than the other competitors.
   (D) illustrate how many newspapers try to increase their readership by sponsoring events.

15. Which of the following best states why the people of Les Landes used stilts?

    (A) Les Landes is an extremely flat area.
    (B) A newspaper was offering a prize for a stilt race.
    (C) The shepherds could see their sheep more easily.
    (D) The land was filled with ditches and marshes.

16. The most likely reason that the author says that the "response from the local people was overwhelming" (lines 18–19) was that

    (A) 75 men entered the race.
    (B) bets were made on who would win.
    (C) the contestants got tired.
    (D) the café owners greeted the competitors.

17. Which of the following most completely gives the reasons that the race was difficult?

    (A) The route was long and covered various types of terrain.
    (B) The route was chosen by the organizers for its many cafés.
    (C) The route was unknown to the participants.
    (D) The route included large areas that were well populated.

18. Which of the following statements best explains "halfway through the race, the field had narrowed to only 32 contestants" (lines 34–35)?

    (A) The course was not as wide as it was at the beginning.
    (B) The marshy land was flooded.
    (C) There were fewer racers.
    (D) Some racers had been cheating.

Passage 2 Questions

19. The main point of this passage is to

    (A) illustrate how many newspapers try to increase their readership by sponsoring events.
    (B) describe the accomplishments of early cyclist Maurice Garin.
    (C) describe how the race was beset with issues of cheating in the early years.
    (D) deliberate on the differences between the first Tour de France and the Tour de France of today.

20. The riders were unscrupulous (line 33). This means that they

    (A) were skilled cyclists.
    (B) had a lot of endurance.
    (C) were very resourceful.
    (D) used dishonest tactics.

21. The most likely reason that the author used the word "shockingly" was because it was surprising that

    (A) Garin won by only one minute.
    (B) it took Garin 17 hours to go 300 miles.
    (C) Garin was the winner.
    (D) that part of the race was so long.

22. It can reasonably be inferred from the passage that

    (A) the allure of fame is what motivated the competitors.
    (B) the prize was a large amount of money at the time.
    (C) there were bad feelings between the winner and the losers.
    (D) the competitors had bonded because of the race.

23. Which of the following was a problem that the racers faced?

    (A) blistering sun
    (B) lack of food
    (C) rain and sleet
    (D) lack of sleep

Paired Passage Questions

24. Unlike in Passage 1, in Passage 2 the author

    (A) is much more cynical about the morals of racers and their fans.
    (B) considers endurance races something that anyone could participate in.
    (C) feels that too much publicity can ruin a race.
    (D) thinks that it is important to have a large reward for endurance races.

25. The authors of Passage 1 and Passage 2 would most likely agree that

    (A) there are many ways to cheat in an endurance race.
    (B) races at the turn of the twentieth century were more difficult than the races of today.
    (C) endurance races are difficult and grueling competitions.
    (D) the celebration at the end of an endurance race is worth all the pain.

26. In both Passage 1 and Passage 2, the impetus for hosting the race is

    (A) to entertain the masses.
    (B) to boost flagging newspaper sales.
    (C) to see how much the human body could endure.
    (D) to showcase the most deserving athlete.

27. In contrast to Passage 2, Passage 1
    (A) has a much more positive outlook on fan interaction with contestants.
    (B) portrays an endurance race as something that the contestants enjoy.
    (C) considers endurance races a time-honored tradition.
    (D) indicates that the race helped the newspaper to boost circulation.

Humanities

Up from Slavery by Booker T. Washington

Booker T. Washington (1856–1915), the first principal of Tuskegee Institute in Alabama, was born into slavery. The following passage is from his autobiography.

The cabin was not only our living-place, but was also used as the kitchen for the plantation. My mother was the plantation cook. The cabin was without glass windows; it had only openings in the side which let in the light, and also the cold, chilly air of winter. There was a door to the cabin—that is, something that was called a door—but the uncertain hinges by which it was hung, and the large cracks in it, to 5 say nothing of the fact that it was too small, made the room a very uncomfortable one.

In addition to these openings there was, in the lower right-hand corner of the room, the "cat-hole,"—a contrivance which almost every mansion or cabin in Virginia possessed during the antebellum period. The "cat-hole" was a square opening, about seven by eight inches, provided for the purpose of letting the cat pass in 10 and out of the house at will during the night. In the case of our particular cabin, I could never understand the necessity for this convenience, since there were at least a half-dozen other places in the cabin that would have accommodated the cats.

There was no wooden floor in our cabin, the naked earth being used as a floor. In the center of the earthen floor there was a large, deep opening covered with 15 boards, which was used as a place in which to store sweet potatoes during the winter. An impression of this potato-hole is very distinctly engraved upon my memory, because I recall that during the process of putting the potatoes in or taking them out, I would often come into possession of one or two, which I roasted and thoroughly enjoyed. There was no cooking-stove on our plantation, and all 20 the cooking for the whites and slaves my mother had to do over an open fireplace, mostly in pots and skillets. While the poorly built cabin caused us to suffer with cold in the winter, the heat from the open fireplace in summer was equally trying.

The early years of my life, which were spent in the little cabin, were not very different from those of thousands of other slaves. My mother, of course, had little 25 time in which to give attention to the training of her children during the day. She snatched a few moments for our care in the early morning before her work began, and at night after the day's work was done. One of my earliest recollections is that of my mother cooking a chicken late at night, and awakening her children for the purpose of feeding them. How or where she got it I do not know. I presume, 30 however, it was procured from our owner's farm. Some people may call this theft. If such a thing were to happen now, I should condemn it as theft myself. But taking place at the time it did, and for the reason that it did, no one could ever make me believe that my mother was guilty of thieving. She was simply a victim of the system of slavery. 35

I cannot remember having slept in a bed until after our family was declared free by the Emancipation Proclamation. Three children—John, my older brother, Amanda, my sister, and myself—had a pallet on the dirt floor, or, to be more correct, we slept in and on a bundle of filthy rags laid upon the dirt floor.

I had no schooling whatever while I was a slave, though I remember on several 40 occasions I went as far as the schoolhouse door with one of my young mistresses to carry her books. The picture of several dozen boys and girls in a schoolroom engaged in study made a deep impression upon me, and I had the feeling that to get into a schoolhouse and study in this way would be about the same as getting into paradise. 45

So far as I can now recall, the first knowledge that I got of the fact that we were slaves, and that freedom of the slaves was being discussed, was early one morning before day, when I was awakened by my mother kneeling over her children and fervently praying that Lincoln and his armies might be successful, and that one day she and her children might be free. 50

In this connection I have never been able to understand how the slaves throughout the South, completely ignorant as were the masses so far as books or newspapers were concerned, were able to keep themselves so accurately and completely informed about the great national questions that were agitating the country. From the time that Garrison, Lovejoy, and others began to agitate for freedom, the slaves 55 throughout the South kept in close touch with the progress of the movement.

Though I was a mere child during the preparation for the Civil War and during the war itself, I now recall the many late-at-night whispered discussions that I heard my mother and the other slaves on the plantation indulge in. These discussions showed that they understood the situation, and that they kept themselves informed 60 of events by what was termed the "grape-vine" telegraph.

28. Which of the following statements explains why Washington did not understand why the cabin had a cat-hole?
    (A) They had no cat.
    (B) The hole was too small for people to pass through.
    (C) There were a number of holes in the walls.
    (D) The sweet potatoes covered it up.

29. It can reasonably be inferred that Washington's early years were
    (A) something he tried to forget.
    (B) free of any major problems.
    (C) a large influence on him.
    (D) difficult to remember.

30. It can reasonably be inferred that Washington told the story of his mother's cooking a chicken so that the reader would

(A) reflect on whether she stole the chicken or not.

(B) understand the desperate situation the family was in.

(C) be sympathetic toward their masters.

(D) realize the difficult work his mother did.

31. In the third paragraph (lines 14–23), the author most nearly characterizes his experience eating sweet potatoes as

(A) a thoughtful moment in his young life.

(B) a funny occurrence that he never forgot.

(C) a fond memory among many depressing ones.

(D) a confusing event that led to his desire to achieve.

32. In the context of the passage, the fifth paragraph (lines 36–39) is best described as

(A) giving the reader a realistic understanding of Washington's living conditions.

(B) comparing the lives of slaves and masters.

(C) complaining to the reader about his life as a child.

(D) being careful how he talks about the conditions that he encountered in the cabin.

33. Based on Washington's experience of seeing the classroom in the sixth paragraph (lines 40–45), it can reasonably be inferred that he thought that school was

(A) beyond his reach.

(B) useful in becoming a lawyer.

(C) something he would be fearful of trying.

(D) a goal he had to attain.

34. Washington discusses many of his earliest memories EXCEPT

(A) what kind of food he ate.

(B) what kind of place he lived in.

(C) what he thought about school.

(D) what his owner's name was.

35. Which aspect of life as a slave seemed most surprising to Washington?

(A) The fact that slaves knew what was going on in the country

(B) The idea that slaves could spend time with their families

(C) The idea that slaves enjoyed talking to each other when they weren't working

(D) The fact that slaves may have stolen from their owners

36. In the last paragraph, Washington refers to the "grape-vine" telegraph (line 61) in order to show

   (A) how unaware the slaves were.
   (B) how hopeful the slaves were.
   (C) how the slaves spent their time.
   (D) how the slaves found things out.

37. The main point of this passage is to

   (A) indicate the results of the Civil War.
   (B) show the harsh realities of the slaves' lives.
   (C) criticize the way Washington's mother treated her children.
   (D) prove that education is valuable.

38. It could reasonably be inferred that the author's attitude toward his past was

   (A) one of anger and resentment.
   (B) one of sensitivity and acceptance.
   (C) one of fear and deception.
   (D) one of indifference and boredom.

39. Why was it possible for Washington to see the schoolhouse?

   (A) He was performing a job for the owner's daughter.
   (B) He was being taught by the teacher who ran the school.
   (C) He was allowed to go to the school and do errands for the teacher.
   (D) He was able to sneak out of the cabin in the early morning.

40. Based on the seventh paragraph (lines 46–50), what effect did Washington's mother's praying have on him?

   (A) It made him want to stand up to his owner.
   (B) It made him realize that he was not free.
   (C) It made him fear his mother.
   (D) It made him want to go to war.

41. When the author speaks of the "cat-hole" as a contrivance (line 8), he means that it was a(n)

   (A) adaptor.
   (B) concession.
   (C) device.
   (D) generator.

Natural Sciences

The Progression of Written Language

Once we learn to write at an early age, we take writing for granted. But as this passage shows, writing has a long and complicated history.

The fact that we can speak to one another and exchange complicated information may seem like a miracle. But if spoken language is a miracle, the ability to write using an alphabet seems almost incredible. Everyone who speaks English knows tens of thousands of words—out of a total of 1,500,000 words in the English language—and all those words can be represented by just 26 letters. 5

How did people ever learn to write? We know that spoken languages existed long before writing was invented. How did people get the idea of representing all the words of a whole language, big words and little words, with just a small number of letters? How did they decide to ignore the tone of voice and pay attention only to the words? Indeed, who got the idea of writing? How did it all begin? 10

No one knows for sure. One theory is that the first writing was employed by rich people to keep track of all their possessions, for example, their sheep and jars of grain. Another theory is that writing was developed as a means of recording payment of taxes. The theory goes like this: a man must pay four jars of wine as his tax. He brings the tax to a tax collector, who has to find a way of recording this 15 information. The tax collector asks a man who keeps the records—a scribe—to record the information that the taxes were paid. The scribe draws four jars of wine. This was the beginning of written language.

After a while, a clever scribe doesn't draw four jars of wine. He draws just one jar and makes four lines under it. Still later, a smart scribe doesn't draw the 20 whole jar; he just draws a mark to stand for the whole jar. At this point, the scribe's record might look like this: ^//// (where ^ stands for "jar" and the four lines stand for "four"). He draws a different mark to stand for "olives," and yet another mark to stand for "wheat." His record for three jars of olives might look like this: *///. The scribe has to remember, of course, what all the marks stand for. 25

In the beginning, scribes agreed on hundreds of pictures or marks that stood for words like *king* or *built* or *jar*. They might learn thousands of word pictures, such as the ones in Egyptian hieroglyphics, which originated about 53 centuries ago. Scribes, who spent years learning this way of writing, were important people, sometimes priestly rulers or well-paid representatives of the king. Some countries 30 had only a few dozen scribes, because the job was so demanding. Of course, anyone who has finished seventh grade today and knows our alphabet would be a lot more skilled at writing than the best scribes of ancient times.

There were some advantages to this kind of written language. Sometimes, people in different parts of the country—or in different countries altogether—spoke 35 different languages. But they could use the same sign for *king* or *jar* or *fight*, so scribes from all parts of the country could communicate, at least a little, in the written language.

This works even today. The language we call Chinese is actually several different languages. But people in China can always communicate through writing, 40 because Chinese writing uses word signs instead of letters that represent sounds. Our own writing system contains a few word signs—numerals, for example. So people in Sweden or Russia can read signs like *4* or *5* as easily as you can. There are also signs for places to sleep or eat and to give warnings on highways that make use of symbols or pictures that people all over the world can recognize. 45

We don't know who made the first alphabet. In the fall of 1999, two scientists published a study of carvings found in an Egyptian desert. They theorized that merchants in the Middle East, in what is now Lebanon, Israel, and Syria, made a very simple alphabet about 3,900 years ago. Instead of taking two years to learn thousands of picture marks, these merchants could learn the new alphabet in less 50 than a week. This was a great discovery. The written language could now be learned by far greater numbers of people.

Alphabets slowly spread to other countries, including Greece. Our modern term *alphabet* is derived from the first two Greek letters, alpha and beta. English words are confusing to spell, because there are only 26 letters to represent 40 55 sounds and because the spelling of many words is based on several other languages that the words come from. Even so, large numbers of people around the world are able to communicate by reading and writing English.

We don't know the identity of the Middle Eastern merchants who developed the simple alphabet, and no one has translated their message yet. We cannot even 60 be sure that other scientific findings in the future won't disprove this whole account of a simple alphabet. We don't know the dates of any of the great inventions in writing, nor the names of any of the early geniuses who developed writing thousands of years ago. But all that is immaterial. What we do know is that writing is an amazing achievement. 65

42. The main point of the passage is that

    (A) writing a language is the same as speaking it.

    (B) all written languages use letters to stand for sounds.

    (C) written languages were invented before spoken languages.

    (D) written language evolved slowly over many years.

43. According to the passage, writing may have developed

    (A) to keep track of possessions.

    (B) to write down religious ceremonies.

    (C) to record the best times to plant and to harvest.

    (D) to record victories of the king and his army.

44. According to the passage, one advantage of using picture symbols for writing rather than an alphabet was that it
    (A) was cheaper.
    (B) used only 26 symbols.
    (C) could be read by people who spoke different languages.
    (D) meant that scribes were important people.

45. According to the fifth paragraph (lines 26–33), scribes were well-paid, important people because they
    (A) were the rulers.
    (B) kept track of collected taxes.
    (C) taught the alphabet to other people.
    (D) could speak many languages.

46. It can reasonably be inferred that scribes began to use symbols instead of pictures because it
    (A) cost less money.
    (B) made more sense.
    (C) looked better.
    (D) was much faster.

47. People in the United States and Sweden can read the numeral 4 because
    (A) the symbol is used in the same way in both countries.
    (B) the Swedish language uses an alphabet.
    (C) Swedish and Russian use the same alphabet.
    (D) people around the world use the English alphabet to communicate.

48. According to the passage, the idea of writing with an alphabet may have first developed in
    (A) China and Japan.
    (B) Lebanon, Israel, and Syria.
    (C) Peru and Mexico.
    (D) Egypt and Greece.

49. According to the passage, the first alphabet was probably invented before
    (A) picture writing.
    (B) the Greek alphabet.
    (C) any spoken language.
    (D) hieroglyphics.

50. It can reasonably be inferred that the language for which a writing system was developed last was

(A) English.
(B) Egyptian.
(C) Greek.
(D) Chinese.

51. According to the passage, why are English words confusing to spell (lines 54–57)?

(A) There are 40 sounds that make up words but only 26 letters in the alphabet.
(B) English was the last language for which a writing system was developed.
(C) English words are very long.
(D) English words are difficult to pronounce.

52. According to the passage, which language uses a writing system based on pictures rather than letters?

(A) Russian
(B) Swedish
(C) English
(D) Chinese

53. It can reasonably be inferred that the author of the passage probably holds the opinion that

(A) knowing how to write creates problems for people.
(B) countries that use picture writing are better than countries that use alphabets.
(C) it is good for people to be able to communicate with one another.
(D) all countries should use the same alphabet.

54. According to the passage, in what way is a writing system of letters superior to a system of pictures?

(A) People can learn an alphabet more quickly than symbols.
(B) An alphabet allows people who speak different languages to understand each other.
(C) People can learn to record information more quickly with an alphabet.
(D) An alphabet has more letters than a system of pictures.

55. When the author states that knowing the names of those who developed writing thousands of years ago is *immaterial* (line 64), the author means that it is

(A) vital to know them.
(B) not easy to know them.
(C) unimportant to know them.
(D) acceptable to know them.

Prose Fiction

"Hearts and Hands" by O. Henry

O. Henry (1862–1910) lived in the American West as a young man. Accused of embezzling money while working in a bank, he began writing while in federal prison. He became famous for short stories with surprise endings. See if the ending of this story surprises you.

At Denver there was an influx of passengers into the coaches on the eastbound express. In one coach there sat a very pretty young woman dressed in elegant taste and surrounded by all the luxurious comforts of an experienced traveler. Among the newcomers were two young men, one of handsome presence with a bold, frank look and manner, the other a ruffled, glum-faced person, heavily built and roughly   5
dressed. The two were handcuffed together.

As they passed down the aisle of the coach, the only vacant seat offered was a reversed one facing the attractive young woman. Here the linked couple seated themselves. The young woman's glance fell upon them with a distant, swift disinterest. Then with a lovely smile brightening her face and a tender pink coloring her   10
rounded cheeks, she held out a little gray-gloved hand. When she spoke her voice, full, sweet, and deliberate, proclaimed that its owner was accustomed to speak and be heard.

"Well, Mr. Easton, if you *will* make me speak first, I suppose I must. Don't you ever recognize old friends when you meet them in the West?"   15

The younger man roused himself sharply at the sound of her voice, seemed to struggle with a slight embarrassment which he threw off instantly, and then clasped her fingers with his left hand.

"It's Miss Fairchild," he said, with a smile. "I'll ask you to excuse the other hand; it's otherwise engaged just at present."   20

He slightly raised his right hand, bound at the wrist by the shining "bracelet" to the left one of his companion. The glad look in the girl's eyes slowly changed to a bewildered horror. The glow faded from her cheeks. Her lips parted in a vague distress. Easton, with a little laugh, as if amused, was about to speak again, when the other man interrupted him. The glum-faced man had been watching the girl's   25
countenance with veiled glances from his keen, shrewd eyes.

"You'll excuse me for speaking, miss, but I see you're acquainted with the marshal here. If you'll ask him to speak a word for me when we get to the pen he'll do it, and it'll make things easier for me there. He's taking me to Leavenworth prison. It's seven years for counterfeiting." 30

"Oh!" said the girl, with a deep breath and returning color. "So that is what you are doing out here? A marshal!"

"My dear Miss Fairchild," said Easton, calmly, "I had to do something. Money has a way of taking wings unto itself, and you know it takes money to keep in step with our crowd in Washington. I saw this opening in the West, and—well, a 35 marshalship isn't quite as high a position as that of ambassador, but—"

"The ambassador," said the girl, warmly, "doesn't call any more. He needn't ever have done so. You ought to know that. And so now you are one of these dashing Western heroes, and you ride and shoot and go into all kinds of dangers. That's different from the Washington life. You have been missed from the old crowd." 40

The girl's eyes, fascinated, went back, widening a little, to rest upon the glittering handcuffs.

"Don't you worry about them, miss," said the other man. "All marshals handcuff themselves to their prisoners to keep them from getting away. Mr. Easton knows his business." 45

"Will we see you again soon in Washington?" asked the girl.

"Not soon, I think," said Easton. "My butterfly days are over, I fear."

"I love the West," said the girl. Her eyes were shining softly. She looked out the car window. She began to speak truly and simply, without the gloss of style and manner: "Mamma and I spent the summer in Denver. She went home a week ago, 50 because Father was slightly ill. I could live and be happy in the West. I think the air here agrees with me. Money isn't everything. But people always misunderstand things and remain stupid—"

"Say, Mr. Marshal," growled the glum-faced man. "This isn't quite fair. I haven't had a smoke all day. Haven't you talked long enough? Take me in the 55 smoker now, won't you? I'm half dead for a pipe."

The bound travelers rose to their feet, Easton with the same slow smile on his face.

"I can't deny a petition for tobacco," he said lightly. "It's the one friend of the unfortunate. Good-bye, Miss Fairchild. Duty calls, you know." He held out his 60 hand for a farewell.

"It's too bad you are not going East," she said, reclothing herself with manner and style. "But you must go on to Leavenworth, I suppose?"

"Yes," said Easton, "I must go on to Leavenworth."

The two men sidled down the aisle into the smoker. 65

The two passengers in a seat nearby had heard most of the conversation. Said one of them: "That marshal's a good sort of chap. Some of these Western fellows are all right."

"Pretty young to hold an office like that, isn't he?" asked the other.

"Young!" exclaimed the first speaker, "why—Oh, didn't you catch on? Say— 70 did you ever know an officer to handcuff a prisoner to his *right* hand?"

56. Based on the information in the introduction, which of the following is most likely true?
    (A) O. Henry was familiar with the foreign service.
    (B) O. Henry knew something about going to prison.
    (C) O. Henry wrote poetry about traveling through the West.
    (D) O. Henry served as marshal in the western United States.

57. In the sixth paragraph (lines 21–26), the *bracelet* worn by Easton was
    (A) a handcuff.
    (B) a present from Miss Fairchild.
    (C) worth a lot of money.
    (D) something only women usually wear.

58. Which of the following is the most likely description of Easton's relationship to the ambassador?
    (A) He was a good friend of the ambassador and misses him.
    (B) He left Washington because he fought with him.
    (C) He wanted to become ambassador instead.
    (D) He was jealous about his seeing Miss Fairchild in Washington.

59. It can reasonably be inferred that Miss Fairchild
    (A) was never interested in Easton.
    (B) would like to see more of Easton.
    (C) thinks Easton has changed a good deal.
    (D) worries that Easton will try to see her more.

60. When the author says that Easton "seemed to struggle with a slight embarrassment" (lines 15–16), he is referring to the fact that Easton was
    (A) a marshal.
    (B) handcuffed.
    (C) unhappy to be on the train.
    (D) displeased with Miss Fairchild.

61. When Easton says, "My butterfly days are over, I fear" (line 47), he means that he
    (A) is no longer popular.
    (B) can no longer be frivolous.
    (C) is busy with traveling.
    (D) has a lot of prisoners he needs to see.

62. Based on the information in the passage, the real reason the older man asks to be taken to the smoking car is that he

   (A) is tired of the conversation.
   (B) wants to save Easton from embarrassment.
   (C) doesn't like Miss Fairchild.
   (D) is trying to escape.

63. In the last paragraph, the significance of the passenger saying "Oh, didn't you catch on?" (line 70) is that it tells the reader that he

   (A) knew that Easton was not the real marshal.
   (B) realized that Easton was really the marshal.
   (C) knew Easton.
   (D) had met Miss Fairchild.

64. When Easton says, "Money has a way of taking wings unto itself" (lines 33–34), he means that he

   (A) is not interested in money.
   (B) saved money in the West.
   (C) has a lot of money.
   (D) spent most of his money.

65. Which of the following statements best describes Miss Fairchild's initial reaction on seeing Easton with handcuffs?

   (A) She was uninterested.
   (B) She thought it was funny.
   (C) She was horrified.
   (D) She was angry.

66. When the author says that the "glum-faced man had been watching the girl's countenance with veiled glances from his keen, shrewd eyes" (lines 25–26), he is suggesting that the man

   (A) was interested in what was going on between Miss Fairchild and Easton.
   (B) was looking for a way to impress Miss Fairchild.
   (C) wanted to tell Miss Fairchild why Easton came to the West.
   (D) thought Miss Fairchild should be careful of Easton.

67. By the end of the story, the reader is able to realize that

   (A) Easton had been in prison for several years.
   (B) Easton was the prisoner.
   (C) Easton never was in Washington.
   (D) Easton does not like Miss Fairchild.

68. Based on his actions in the passage, the glum-faced man can be best described as

(A) compassionate.
(B) detached.
(C) malicious.
(D) squeamish.

69. The first three paragraphs (lines 1–15) establish all of the following about Miss Fairchild EXCEPT

(A) what she looks like.
(B) why she is on the train.
(C) that she knows Easton.
(D) that she is well-mannered.

CHAPTER 2

Set 2 Reading Questions

Prose Fiction

"Mr. Travers's First Hunt" by Richard Harding Davis

Richard Harding Davis (1864–1916) wrote humorous short stories about people who were rich enough to own dogs and horses for the sport of fox hunting. This is an adaptation of one story.

Young Travers, who had been engaged to a girl down on Long Island, only met her father and brother a few weeks before the day set for the wedding. The father and son talked about horses all day and until one in the morning, for they owned fast thoroughbreds, and entered them at race-tracks. Old Mr. Paddock, the father of the girl to whom Travers was 5 engaged, had often said that when a young man asked him for his daughter's hand he would ask him in return, not if he had lived straight, but if he could ride straight.

Travers had met Miss Paddock and her mother in Europe, while the men of the family were at home. He was invited to their place in the fall 10 when the fox-hunting season opened, and spent the evening most pleasantly and satisfactorily with his fiancée in a corner of the drawing-room.

But as soon as the women had gone, young Paddock joined him and said, "You ride, of course?" Travers had never ridden; but he had been prompted how to answer by Miss Paddock, and so said there was nothing 15 he liked better.

"That's good," said Paddock. "I'll give you Monster tomorrow morning at the meet. He is a bit nasty at the start of the season; and ever since he killed Wallis, the second groom, last year, none of us care much to ride him. But you can manage him, no doubt." 20

Mr. Travers dreamed that night of taking large, desperate leaps into space on a wild horse that snorted forth flames, and that rose at solid stone walls as though they were haystacks.

He was tempted to say he was ill in the morning—which was, considering his state of mind, more or less true—but concluded that, as he would have to ride sooner or later during his visit, and that if he did break his neck, it would be in a good cause, he determined to do his best.

He came downstairs looking very miserable indeed. Monster had been taken to the place where they were to meet, and Travers viewed him on his arrival there with a sickening sense of fear as he saw him pulling three grooms off their feet.

Travers decided that he would stay with his feet on solid earth just as long as he could, and when the hounds were sent off and the rest had started at a gallop, he waited until they were all well away. Then he scrambled up onto the saddle. His feet fell quite by accident into the stirrups, and the next instant he was off after the others, with a feeling that he was on a locomotive that was jumping the ties. Monster had passed the other horses in less than five minutes.

Travers had taken hold of the saddle with his left hand to keep himself down, and sawed and swayed on the reins with his right. He shut his eyes whenever Monster jumped, and never knew how he happened to stick on; but he did stick on, and was so far ahead that no one could see in the misty morning just how badly he rode. As it was, for daring and speed he led the field, and not even young Paddock was near him from the start.

There was a broad stream in front of him, and a hill just on its other side. No one had ever tried to take this at a jump. It was considered more of a swim than anything else, and the hunters always crossed it by the bridge, towards the left. Travers saw the bridge and tried to jerk Monster's head in that direction; but Monster kept right on as straight as an express train over the prairie.

Travers could only gasp and shut his eyes. He remembered the fate of the second groom and shivered. Then the horse rose like a rocket, lifting Travers so high in the air that he thought Monster would never come down again; but he did come down, on the opposite side of the stream. The next instant he was up and over the hill, and had stopped panting in the very center of the pack of hounds that were snarling and snapping around the fox.

And then Travers showed that he was a thoroughbred, even though he could not ride, for he hastily fumbled for his cigar case, and when the others came pounding up over the bridge and around the hill, they saw him seated nonchalantly on his saddle, puffing critically at a cigar, and giving Monster patronizing pats on the head.

"My dear girl," said old Mr. Paddock to his daughter as they rode back, "if you love that young man of yours and want to keep him, make him promise to give up riding. A more reckless and more brilliant horseman I have never seen. He took that jump at that stream like a centaur. But he will break his neck sooner or later, and he ought to be stopped."

Young Paddock was so delighted with his prospective brother-in-law's great riding that that night in the smoking-room he made him a present of Monster before all the men.

"No," said Travers, gloomily, "I can't take him. Your sister has asked me to give up what is dearer to me than anything next to herself, and that is my riding. She has asked me to promise never to ride again, and I have given my word."

A chorus of sympathy rose from the men.

"Yes, I know," said Travers to her brother, "it is rough, but it just shows what sacrifices a man will make for the woman he loves."

70

70. The point of view from which the passage is told can best be described as that of

    (A) a narrator who rode with Travers on the fox hunt.

    (B) a narrator who is aware of Travers's problem.

    (C) a narrator who is a member of the Paddock family.

    (D) a narrator who has no riding ability.

71. Which of the following statements best indicates why Travers tells his future brother-in-law that he likes to ride horses?

    (A) He is an excellent horseman.

    (B) His fiancée told him to say that.

    (C) He wants to ride in the fox hunt.

    (D) He likes a challenge.

72. All of the following are reasons to fear riding Monster EXCEPT

    (A) that Travers had never ridden a horse.

    (B) that Monster had killed a groom.

    (C) that young Paddock gave Monster to Travers.

    (D) that young Paddock said that Monster was nasty.

73. It can reasonably be inferred that Travers had the dream described in the fifth paragraph (lines 21–23) because he

    (A) was anxious about getting married.

    (B) was afraid of riding Monster.

    (C) had a fever.

    (D) had indigestion from the food he ate at dinner.

74. Which of the following statements best describes Travers's predicament?

    (A) He was worried that his fiancée didn't really care for him.

    (B) He was fearful of asking young Paddock how to ride.

    (C) He wanted to impress young Paddock, but he didn't know how.

    (D) He wanted to impress his fiancée's family, but he was afraid.

75. Travers gives the impression that he is a great rider by

    (A) managing to stay on Monster as the horse goes wildly onward.

    (B) showing that he is skilled in handling the horse.

    (C) getting Monster to do several jumps.

    (D) bragging a lot about his riding ability after the hunt.

76. Which of the following statements best explains why Travers did not take the bridge over the stream?

    (A) He preferred to jump over it.

    (B) He couldn't get Monster to go over to it.

    (C) He wanted to show off his courage and skill.

    (D) His fiancée warned him not to.

77. When the author says that Travers felt as though "he was on a locomotive that was jumping the ties" (line 35), he means that Travers

    (A) realized that the horse was galloping.

    (B) could not control the horse.

    (C) was getting hurt.

    (D) was enjoying the ride.

78. In the fourth paragraph (lines 17–20), what is one probable reason that young Paddock chooses Monster for Travers to ride?

    (A) He thinks Travers deserves the best horse.

    (B) He wants to upset his sister.

    (C) He wants to please Travers.

    (D) He wants to test Travers.

79. When the author says that Monster "rose like a rocket" (line 49), he means that the horse

    (A) went up in the air with a great force.

    (B) made a loud sound.

    (C) went up in the air slowly at first.

    (D) was startled.

80. The sacrifice that Travers refers to in the last paragraph is most likely

    (A) that he had to ride Monster.

    (B) that he had decided to marry.

    (C) that he was starting a new life.

    (D) that he was giving up Monster.

81. When the author says that after Monster came to a stop, the others found Travers seated *nonchalantly* on his saddle (lines 56–57), he means that Travers

    (A) looked like a great horseman.

    (B) acted unconcerned.

    (C) acted nervously.

    (D) worked hard to keep control.

82. It can reasonably be inferred that this story is

(A) highly improbable.

(B) filled with significant meaning.

(C) very moral.

(D) extremely serious.

83. Which of the following descriptions best characterizes Travers?

(A) Delusional and irrational

(B) Full of regret for what he pretended to be

(C) Intelligent and predictable

(D) Willing to try anything in order to please others

Social Sciences

"I Have a Dream" by Martin Luther King Jr.

This is an excerpt from the famous speech that Martin Luther King Jr. (1929–1968) gave on August 28, 1963 in Washington, DC, before a quarter of a million supporters of his civil rights stance.

Five score years ago, a great American, in whose symbolic shadow we stand, signed the Emancipation Proclamation. This momentous decree came as a great beacon light of hope to millions of Negro slaves who had been seared in the flames of withering injustice. It came as a joyous daybreak to end the long night of captivity.   5

But one hundred years later, we must face the tragic fact that the Negro is still not free. One hundred years later, the life of the Negro is still sadly crippled by the manacles of segregation and the chains of discrimination. One hundred years later, the Negro lives on a lonely island of poverty in the midst of a vast ocean of material prosperity. One hundred years later, the Negro is still languishing in the corners of   10 American society and finds himself an exile in his own land. So we have come here today to dramatize an appalling condition.

In a sense we have come to our nation's capital to cash a check. When the architects of our republic wrote the magnificent words of the Constitution and the Declaration of Independence, they were signing a promissory note to which every 15 American was to fall heir. This note was a promise that all men would be guaranteed the inalienable rights of life, liberty, and the pursuit of happiness.

It is obvious today that America has defaulted on this promissory note insofar as her citizens of color are concerned. Instead of honoring this sacred obligation, America has given the Negro people a bad check which has come back marked 20 "insufficient funds." But we refuse to believe that the bank of justice is bankrupt. We refuse to believe that there are insufficient funds in the great vaults of opportunity of this nation. So we have come to cash this check—a check that will give us upon demand the riches of freedom and the security of justice. We have also

come to this hallowed spot to remind America of the fierce urgency of now. This is 25
no time to engage in the luxury of cooling off or to take the tranquilizing drug of
gradualism. Now is the time to rise from the dark and desolate valley of segregation
to the sunlit path of racial justice. Now is the time to open the doors of opportunity to all of God's children. Now is the time to lift our nation from the quicksands
of racial injustice to the solid rock of brotherhood. . . . 30

I am not unmindful that some of you have come here out of great trials and
tribulations. Some of you have come fresh from narrow cells. Some of you have
come from areas where your quest for freedom left you battered by the storms of
persecution and staggered by the winds of police brutality. You have been the vet-
erans of creative suffering. Continue to work with the faith that unearned suffering 35
is redemptive.

Go back to Mississippi, go back to Alabama, go back to Georgia, go back to
Louisiana, go back to the slums and ghettos of our northern cities, knowing that
somehow this situation can and will be changed. Let us not wallow in the valley
of despair. 40

I say to you today, my friends, that in spite of the difficulties and frustrations of
the moment, I still have a dream. It is a dream deeply rooted in the American dream.

I have a dream that one day this nation will rise up and live out the true meaning
of its creed: "We hold these truths to be self-evident: that all men are created equal."

I have a dream that one day on the red hills of Georgia the sons of former slaves 45
and the sons of former slave owners will be able to sit down together at a table of
brotherhood.

I have a dream that one day even the state of Mississippi, a desert state, swelter-
ing with the heat of injustice and oppression, will be transformed into an oasis of
freedom and justice. 50

I have a dream that my four children will one day live in a nation where they
will not be judged by the color of their skin but by the content of their character.

I have a dream today.

I have a dream that one day the state of Alabama, whose governor's lips are presently dripping with the words of interposition and nullification, will be transformed 55
into a situation where little black boys and black girls will be able to join hands with
little white boys and white girls and walk together as sisters and brothers.

I have a dream today.

I have a dream that one day every valley shall be exalted, every hill and mountain shall be made low, the rough places will be made plain, and the crooked places 60
will be made straight, and the glory of the Lord shall be revealed, and all flesh shall
see it together.

This is our hope. This is the faith with which I return to the South. With this
faith we will be able to hew out of the mountain of despair a stone of hope. With
this faith we will be able to transform the jangling discords of our nation into 65
a beautiful symphony of brotherhood. With this faith we will be able to work
together, to pray together, to struggle together, to go to jail together, to stand up
for freedom together, knowing that we will be free one day.

This will be the day when all of God's children will be able to sing with a new meaning, "My country, 'tis of thee, sweet land of liberty, of thee I sing. Land where my fathers died, land of the pilgrim's pride, from every mountainside, let freedom ring." 70

84. The main point of the second paragraph (lines 6–12) is to
   (A) determine the meaning of freedom.
   (B) recount the way in which slavery was eradicated.
   (C) illustrate the ways in which prejudice is manifested.
   (D) show that race issues were not resolved by the end of slavery.

85. When King says that Negro slaves were "seared in the flames of withering injustice" (lines 3–4), he means that slaves were
   (A) unpaid.
   (B) treated cruelly.
   (C) went to jail very often.
   (D) expected to be loyal.

86. According to the second paragraph (lines 6–12), what was the purpose of the demonstration?
   (A) King wants to make the public aware of the injustices that exist.
   (B) King wants to incite the public into taking action.
   (C) King wants to meet with the governors of the southern states to talk.
   (D) King hopes to raise funds to create grants for those in need.

87. Which of the following sentences from the speech best supports the idea that King has hope for a better world?
   (A) It came as a joyous daybreak to end the long night of captivity.
   (B) It is obvious today that America has defaulted on this promissory note insofar as her citizens of color are concerned.
   (C) Continue to work with the faith that unearned suffering is redemptive.
   (D) With this faith we will be able to transform the jangling discords of our nation into a beautiful symphony of brotherhood.

88. When King says, "One hundred years later, the life of the Negro is still sadly crippled by the manacles of segregation and the chains of discrimination" (lines 7–8), he is comparing segregation and discrimination to being
   (A) in a hospital.
   (B) tied to work.
   (C) in jail.
   (D) kept safe.

89. In the third paragraph, what does King suggest by his use of the word *architects* (line 14)?

  (A) The founders of the United States enjoyed designing buildings.
  (B) Most of the buildings in the country were built by slaves.
  (C) The writers of the Constitution and Declaration designed and built the country.
  (D) The people in charge of bureaucracy built the country.

90. Based on the information in the fourth paragraph (lines 18–30), it can reasonably be inferred that King wanted to

  (A) quickly make changes in civil rights.
  (B) slowly change the way blacks are treated.
  (C) keep segregation as the law of the country.
  (D) hold a countrywide vote on civil rights.

91. Which of the following statements best describes the meaning of the last two lines of the fifth paragraph (lines 35–36)?

  (A) Continue, knowing that suffering is productive.
  (B) Continue, knowing that suffering is evil.
  (C) Continue, knowing that you have faith.
  (D) Continue, knowing that suffering is godly.

92. When King says, "Let us not wallow in the valley of despair" (lines 39–40), he means that he

  (A) does not want his supporters to stumble.
  (B) is encouraging his supporters to go back to their homes.
  (C) does not want his supporters to be self-indulgent.
  (D) wants the situation to change.

93. King mentions the many hardships that African-Americans endure EXCEPT

  (A) returning to slums in the northern cities.
  (B) experiencing police brutality.
  (C) enduring years of racial injustice.
  (D) still not being free.

94. When King says, "It is a dream deeply rooted in the American dream" (line 42), he means that

  (A) his dream is difficult to understand.
  (B) the American dream is the same as the African-American's dream.
  (C) like the American dream, his dream is of freedom.
  (D) his dream is of returning to the South.

95. It can reasonably be inferred from the thirteenth paragraph (lines 54–57) that

(A) there is little hope for progress in Alabama.
(B) the governor of Alabama wants white and black children to play together.
(C) there is blood on the governor's lips.
(D) the governor in Alabama intends to block any progress toward King's dream.

96. The phrase "hew out of the mountain of despair a stone of hope" (line 64) is best described as creating a metaphor for

(A) a step toward freedom.
(B) a symbolic sculpture.
(C) the work that needs to be done.
(D) the impossibility of what King wants to have happen.

97. The last paragraph suggests that

(A) King feels that music is liberating.
(B) the words of the patriotic song will finally apply to all Americans.
(C) children need to learn the meaning of the song.
(D) the song will take on a new and different meaning.

Paired Passages: Humanities

Passage 1: *The Story of My Life* by Helen Keller

Helen Keller (1880–1968) became deaf and blind as the result of an illness at the age of 19 months. In the following adapted passage from her autobiography, she describes how she learned to communicate despite her disabilities, with the help of her teacher, Anne Sullivan. Keller went on to attend college, write several books, and work in many programs to help people.

The morning after my teacher came, she led me into her room and gave me a doll. When I had played with it a little while, Miss Sullivan slowly spelled into my hand the word "d-o-l-l." I was at once interested in this finger play and tried to imitate it. When I finally succeeded in making the letters correctly, I was flushed with childish pleasure and pride. 5

Running downstairs to my mother, I held up my hand and made the letters for doll. I did not know that I was spelling a word or even that words existed; I was simply making my fingers go in monkey-like imitation. In the days that followed I learned to spell in this uncomprehending way a great many words, among them pin, hat, cup, and a few verbs like sit, stand, and walk. But my teacher had been 10 with me several weeks before I understood that everything has a name.

One day, while I was playing with my new doll, Miss Sullivan put my big rag doll into my lap also, spelled "d-o-l-l" and tried to make me understand that "d-o-l-l" applied to both. Earlier in the day we had had a tussle over the words "m-u-g" and "w-a-t-e-r." Miss Sullivan had tried to impress it upon me that "m-u-g" is mug and that "w-a-t-e-r" is water, but I persisted in confounding the two. In despair she had dropped the subject for the time. She brought me my hat, and I knew I was going out into the warm sunshine. This thought, if a word-less sensation may be called a thought, made me hop and skip with pleasure.

We walked down the path to the well-house, attracted by the fragrance of the honeysuckle with which it was covered. Someone was drawing water, and my teacher placed my hand under the spout. As the cool stream gushed over one hand she spelled into the other the word water first slowly, then rapidly. I stood still, my whole attention fixed upon the motions of her fingers. Suddenly I felt a misty consciousness as of something forgotten—a thrill of returning thought; and somehow the mystery of language was revealed to me. I knew then that "w-a-t-e-r" meant the wonderful cool something that was flowing over my hand. That living word awakened my soul, gave it light, hope, joy, set it free! There were barriers still, it is true, but barriers that could in time be swept away.

I left the well-house eager to learn. Everything had a name, and each name gave birth to a new thought. As we returned to the house, every object which I touched seemed to quiver with life. That was because I saw everything with the strange, new sight that had come to me.

I learned a great many new words that day. It would have been difficult to find a happier child than I was as I lay in my crib at the close of that eventful day and lived over the joys it had brought me, and for the first time longed for a new day to come.

Passage 2: *American Notes* by Charles Dickens

The following passage is adapted from *American Notes* by Charles Dickens. It is about a girl named Laura Bridgman who became blind and deaf and lost her sense of smell at 20 months old after a severe illness. In 1837, when she was seven, Samuel Howe heard of her condition and took her to an institution where he could help her learn. This passage is told through Howe's perspective:

The first experiments with Laura were made by taking articles in common use—such as knives, forks, spoons, and keys—and pasting upon them labels with their names printed in raised letters. These she felt very carefully, and soon, of course, distinguished that the crooked lines "spoon" differed as much from the crooked lines "key" as the spoon differed from the key in form.

Then small detached labels, with the same words printed upon them, were put into her hands; and she soon observed that they were similar to the ones pasted on the articles. She showed her perception of this similarity by laying the label "key" upon the key, and the label "spoon" upon the spoon. She was encouraged here by the natural sign of approbation, patting on the head.

The same process was then repeated with all the articles which she could handle, and she very easily learned to place the proper labels upon them. It was evident, however, that the only intellectual exercise was that of imitation and memory. She recollected that the label "book" was placed upon a book, and she repeated the process first from imitation, next from memory, with only the motive of love of approbation, but apparently without the intellectual perception of any relation between the things.

After a while, instead of labels, the individual letters were given to her on detached bits of paper. These were arranged side by side so as to spell "book," "key," etc. Next, they were mixed up in a heap and a sign was made for her to arrange them herself so as to express the words "book," "key," etc. and she did so.

Hitherto, the process had been mechanical, and the success about as great as teaching a very knowing dog a variety of tricks. The poor child had sat in mute amazement, and patiently imitated everything her teacher did; but now the truth began to flash upon her. Her intellect began to work. She perceived that here was a way by which she could herself make up a sign of anything that was in her own mind and show it to another mind. At once her countenance lighted up with a human expression; it was no longer a dog, or parrot; it was an immortal spirit, eagerly seizing upon a new link of union with other spirits! I could almost fix upon the moment when this truth dawned upon her mind, and spread its light to her countenance. I saw that the great obstacle was overcome.

Passage 1 Questions

98. The main point of the passage is to

(A) show that the author liked playing with dolls.

(B) argue against funding to educate the disabled.

(C) persuade people to support laws regarding disabilities.

(D) describe an important event in the author's life.

99. When Keller writes that she "persisted in confounding" (line 16) the words "mug" and "water," she means that she

(A) understood them.

(B) confused them.

(C) worried about them.

(D) could write them.

100. When Helen says, "There were barriers still, it is true, but barriers that could in time be swept away" (lines 28–29), she is most likely referring to

(A) her future teachers.

(B) the way in which she thought about her teacher.

(C) her feeling of closeness to her family.

(D) her future success in life.

101. According to the passage, Helen began to comprehend language when she

(A) was shown the difference between "mug" and "water."
(B) realized the substance that poured from the spout was water.
(C) spelled the word doll into her mother's hand.
(D) began to care about her teacher.

102. In the last part of the passage, the author most nearly characterizes her experience of learning the names of things as

(A) an impossible feat.
(B) an upsetting moment.
(C) an inevitability.
(D) an extraordinary event.

Passage 2 Questions

103. The main point of the passage is

(A) to describe the awakening of a mind in darkness.
(B) to teach people how to deal with someone with disabilities.
(C) to show the similarities between training an animal and training a human.
(D) to illustrate what a brilliant teacher Samuel Howe was.

104. Which of the following statements is most likely the reason the author says "Hitherto, the process had been mechanical, and the success about as great as teaching a very knowing dog a variety of tricks." (lines 22–23)?

(A) He wanted to show that she was very easy to teach.
(B) He wanted to illustrate how well he had been able to teach her tricks.
(C) He wanted to illustrate that she was not using higher intelligence.
(D) He wanted to explain his relationship with his student.

105. The second paragraph of the passage implies that

(A) Laura liked her teacher.
(B) Laura liked to be patted on the head.
(C) Laura's gift for learning was remarkable.
(D) Laura enjoyed playing with spoons.

106. It can reasonably be inferred from the passage that

(A) labeling things is the best way to teach a blind person to read.
(B) learning to read is the gateway to the soul.
(C) Samuel Howe was a kind and devoted man.
(D) being given the ability to communicate with others ignited Laura's intellect.

107. It can reasonably be inferred from the passage that as a teacher Samuel Howe was

(A) structured and persistent.
(B) lenient and careless.
(C) misinformed and erratic.
(D) kind and loving.

Paired Passage Questions

108. The tone of Passage 1 when compared to Passage 2 could be said to be

(A) technical as opposed to personal.
(B) personal as opposed to impersonal.
(C) sorrowful as opposed to happy.
(D) detached as opposed to remorseful.

109. Which choice best states the relationship between the two passages?

(A) Passage 2 challenges the primary argument of Passage 1.
(B) Passage 2 gives an alternate view of an experience similar to that described in Passage 1.
(C) Passage 2 advocates the method described in Passage 1.
(D) Passage 2 explains the process described in Passage 1.

110. Unlike in Passage 2, Passage 1's author uses

(A) similes and metaphors to make her point.
(B) a step-by-step process to show growth.
(C) internal feelings to explain her transformation.
(D) a description of techniques to show the student's progression.

111. In both passages, the pivotal moment is

(A) when the girls are introduced to their teachers.
(B) when the girls spell their first words.
(C) when the girls learn that they can use words to express meaning.
(D) when the girls are allowed to go outside.

Natural Sciences

Left-Handed in a Right-Handed World

It's an everyday question: Why are some people left-handed and others right-handed? Scientists haven't been able to determine the answer. Meanwhile, there are problems and opportunities for the minority of people who are left-handed. This passage presents what we know today about handedness.

About 90 percent of the world's people are right-handed. The criterion employed by scientists who study handedness is which hand a person uses to throw a ball, saw, sew, shoot marbles, cut with a knife, bowl, or strike with a hammer. Fewer than 10 percent of people studied perform all of these activities with their left hand—the genuine lefties of the world. A few people have no handedness 5 preference, freely using either hand as convenience dictates.

Scientists who study this phenomenon are unable to agree on the etiology of hand preference. Renowned geneticist Dr. A. Klar, interviewed in spring 2000, argued that right-handedness is almost entirely determined by traits inherited from one's parents. Dr. Stanley Coren, a prominent psychologist who has studied many 10 left-handed people, disagrees with the inheritance point of view. He thinks that mild brain injury causes people to grow up with a preference for the left hand. And still other scientists, like Daniel Geschwind, feel that the traits you are born with, plus your parents' preferences, plus injury, plus early events in your life must all be taken into account to determine handedness. 15

While we know little about what causes people to prefer the left hand, we know several interesting facts about left-handed people. Although no careful statistical studies of the success rate of lefties vs. righties have ever been published, informal observation suggests that lefties are often leaders in their fields. Most recent American presidents have been left-handed. Many of the most successful sports 20 figures have been left-handed, including Babe Ruth, the home-run hitter who was also a great pitcher and was named the greatest athlete of the last hundred years.

Left-handed people are dominant in many fields. World conquerors like Alexander the Great, Julius Caesar, and Napoleon, and the two most glamorous actresses of the twentieth century, Marilyn Monroe and Greta Garbo, were lefties. 25 Leonardo da Vinci, Raphael, and Michelangelo are often called our greatest artists, Beethoven our greatest musician, Mark Twain our most popular writer, and Albert Einstein our greatest scientist. All were lefties. And then there's Paul McCartney of the Beatles, baseball star Ted Williams, tennis stars Monica Seles and John McEnroe, and Benjamin Franklin and Helen Keller. Left-handed television and 30 film performers include Jay Leno, Julia Roberts, Bruce Willis, Tom Cruise, Robert De Niro, Angelina Jolie, and Whoopi Goldberg. Even renowned criminals like Billy the Kid and John Dillinger were lefties.

Left-handedness runs in families. In the British royal family, Queen Elizabeth, Prince Charles, and Prince William are lefties. The Kerr clan in Scotland suppos- 35 edly had so many lefties that their castles were built with counterclockwise spiral stairways, which someone who held a sword in his left hand could defend more easily. Several scientists are busily analyzing blood samples of parents and children to identify genetic markers of handedness. More men (12.6 percent) are left-handed than women (9.9 percent), and left-handedness is found less often among 40 Asians and Hispanics than among whites, blacks, and Native Americans.

Some people don't want their children to grow up left-handed, because so many tools and apparatus are made for right-handed people. They tie the child's left hand behind its back, where it can't be used, thereby forcing the child to use the right

hand, which consequently grows stronger. This procedure is usually effective in 45
shifting competence and power to the right hand, but scientists are almost unanimous in arguing against this technique. Either hand is satisfactory, and no child
should be forced to change against its will. In some cases, being left-handed may
be an advantage. Baseball players think that left-handed batters have an advantage,
since pitchers aren't used to pitching to lefties. 50

An organization of lefties exists to help children deal with the many minor
problems connected with growing up slightly different from other people. It's
called Left-Handers International, and membership is free for lefties. The club
provides a magazine, books on topics such as how to play the guitar left-handed,
and left-handed playing cards, scissors, and toothbrushes. You can join the pen 55
club and correspond with lefties all over the world. There are also many organizations for left-handed adults, and many stores stock products specifically devoted
to people who favor the left hand. The phone book lists 60 American companies
that specialize in the manufacture of leftie products; the most popular products are
cooking utensils and scissors. 60

A right-handed person may gain some understanding of the problems lefties
have in daily life by trying to write with the left hand in a spiral-bound notebook
or at a desk with a writing arm on the right side. A computer can solve most writing problems for a lefty—but you must first change the mouse from right-hand to
left-hand operation. Many power tools are built for right-handed operation. It can 65
be dangerous for a left-handed person to use such a tool with the right hand, since
he or she is less skillful using the right hand.

Many scientific efforts are underway to determine the causative factors in
handedness. Within the next 50 years, we will probably learn more about what
makes people lefties than we learned in the last 2,000 years. 70

112. When the author says in the first paragraph that "a few people have no
handedness preference, freely using either hand as convenience dictates"
(lines 5–6), the author means that

  (A) a few people want to impress their friends with their abilities.
  (B) some people are happier using the left hand.
  (C) these people can use either hand to write and work with.
  (D) some people are not good with either hand.

113. As used in the second paragraph (lines 7–15), *etiology* can best be
defined as

  (A) custom.
  (B) essence.
  (C) effect.
  (D) cause.

114. The third paragraph (lines 16–22) suggests that

    (A) left-handed people live happier lives.
    (B) the causes of hand preference are still undetermined.
    (C) too much effort is devoted to the topic of handedness.
    (D) musicians are usually left-handed.

115. The main point of the fourth paragraph (lines 23–33) is that

    (A) people who are left-handed often excel at what they do.
    (B) left-handedness runs in families.
    (C) most recent American presidents have been left-handed.
    (D) a majority of actors are left-handed.

116. In the fifth paragraph (lines 34–41), what is the most likely reason the author included information about Queen Elizabeth?

    (A) To show that there are left-handed people who are royal
    (B) To try to convince people that being left-handed is not a liability
    (C) To indicate that royals are closely related
    (D) To give an example of how left-handedness is hereditary

117. The author would probably agree with all of the following statements EXCEPT that

    (A) left-handedness is hereditary.
    (B) left-handed people can reach high office.
    (C) most lefties have trouble using computers.
    (D) many great artists, athletes, and criminals have been left-handed.

118. According to the passage, the theory that a preference for the right hand is largely inherited is associated with

    (A) Daniel Geschwind.
    (B) Dr. Stanley Coren.
    (C) Dr. A. Klar.
    (D) Albert Einstein.

119. Based on the information in the passage, which of the following statements is true?

    (A) More people are left-handed than right-handed.
    (B) Most people are right-handed.
    (C) Many people can use both hands equally well.
    (D) Many people are changed from being left-handed.

120. According to the passage, how do most scientists view trying to change a left-handed child to a right-handed one?

(A) They worry that the child will become confused if the handedness is changed from left to right.
(B) They almost completely oppose the practice.
(C) Most think it is best to leave the child alone, although they realize that lefties have a harder time of it.
(D) They feel it may be justified in some cases, such as when a parent wants the child to become a doctor or scientist.

121. According to the passage, left-handed people are as skilled as right-handed people at all of the following EXCEPT

(A) cooking.
(B) playing the guitar.
(C) working on a computer.
(D) using a power tool.

122. According to the passage, which of the following factors is important to scientists in deciding whether a person is right-handed or left-handed?

(A) Which leg the person kicks with
(B) Which hand the person sews with
(C) Which hand is most bitten, if the person bites his or her nails
(D) Which hand is larger

123. Based on the information in the passage, it could reasonably be inferred that left-handed people

(A) have large families.
(B) have trouble using ordinary scissors.
(C) dislike sports.
(D) are more intelligent than right-handed people.

124. Based on the information in the seventh paragraph (lines 51–60), it can reasonably be inferred that

(A) making products for left-handed people is profitable.
(B) many products cannot be changed to accommodate left-handed people.
(C) life for left-handed people is less enjoyable than for right-handed people.
(D) many people feel that left-handedness is a liability.

125. According to the passage, which of the following could schools do to make life easier for left-handed students?

(A) Seat left-handed students together in the classroom.
(B) Provide desks with writing arms on the left side.
(C) Allow left-handed students more leeway when it comes to homework.
(D) Invest in a counselor to meet with left-handed students.

CHAPTER 3

Set 3 Reading Questions

Prose Fiction

"The Lottery Ticket" by Anton Chekhov

The following passage is adapted from a short story written by the Russian author and playwright Anton Chekhov (1860–1904).

Ivan Dmitritch, a middle-class man who lived with his family and was very well satisfied with his lot, sat down on the sofa after supper and began reading the newspaper.

"I forgot to look at the newspaper today," his wife said to him as she cleared the table. "Look and see whether the list of drawings is there."   5

"Yes, it is," said Ivan Dmitritch.

"What is the number?"

"Series 9,499, number 26."

"All right . . . we will look . . . 9,499 and 26."

Ivan Dmitritch had no faith in lottery luck, and would not, as a rule,   10
have consented to look at the lists of winning numbers, but now, as he had nothing else to do and as the newspaper was before his eyes, he passed his finger downwards along the column of numbers. And immediately, as though in mockery of his skepticism, his eye was caught by the figure 9,499! Unable to believe his eyes, he hurriedly dropped the paper on his   15
knees without looking to see the number of the ticket!

"Masha, 9,499 is there!" he said in a hollow voice.

His wife looked at his astonished and panic-stricken face, and realized that he was not joking.

"9,499?" she asked, turning pale and dropping the folded tablecloth   20
on the table.

"Yes, yes . . . it really is there!"

"And the number of the ticket?"

"Oh yes! There's the number of the ticket too. But stay . . . wait! No, I say! Anyway, the number of our series is there!   25

Looking at his wife, Ivan Dmitritch gave a broad, senseless smile, like a baby when a bright object is shown it. His wife smiled too; it was as pleasant to her as to him that he only mentioned the series, and did not try to find out the number of the winning ticket. To torment and tantalize oneself with hopes of possible fortune is so sweet, so thrilling! 30

"It is our series," said Ivan Dmitritch, after a long silence. "So there is a probability that we have won. It's only a probability, but there it is!"

"Well, now look!"

"Wait a little. We have plenty of time to be disappointed. The prize is seventy-five thousand. And in a minute I shall look at the list. I say, what if we 35 really have won?"

The husband and wife began laughing and staring at one another in silence. The possibility of winning bewildered them; they could not have said, could not have dreamed, what they both needed that seventy-five thousand for, what they would buy, where they would go. 40

"And if we have won," he said—"why, it will be a new life, it will be a transformation! The ticket is yours, but if it were mine I should, first of all, of course, spend twenty-five thousand on real property in the shape of an estate; ten thousand on immediate expenses, new furnishings . . . traveling . . . paying debts, and so on. . . . The other forty thousand I would put in the bank and get interest on it." 45

And pictures came crowding on his imagination, each more gracious and poetical than the last. And in all these pictures he saw himself well-fed, serene, healthy, felt warm, even hot!

"Yes, it would be nice to buy an estate," said his wife, also dreaming, and from her face it was evident that she was enchanted by her thoughts. 50

Ivan Dmitritch pictured to himself autumn with its rains and its cold evenings. At that season he would have to take longer walks about the garden and beside the river, so as to get thoroughly chilled. It rains day and night, the bare trees weep, the wind is damp and cold. It is dreary!

Ivan Dmitritch stopped and looked at his wife. 55

"I should go abroad, you know, Masha," he said.

And he began thinking how nice it would be in late autumn to go abroad somewhere to the South of France . . . to Italy . . . to India!

"I should certainly go abroad too," his wife said. "But look at the number of the ticket!" 60

"Wait, wait! . . ."

He walked about the room and went on thinking. It occurred to him: what if his wife really did go abroad? Ivan Dmitritch imagined his wife on the train with a multitude of parcels, baskets, and bags; she would be sighing over something, complaining that the train made her head ache, that she had spent so much 65 money. . . .

"She would begrudge me every farthing," he thought, with a glance at his wife. "The lottery ticket is hers, not mine! She would shut herself up in the hotel, and not let me out of her sight . . . I know!"

And for the first time in his life his mind dwelt on the fact that his wife had 70
grown elderly and plain, while he was still young, fresh, and healthy.

And he looked at his wife, not with a smile now, but with hatred. She glanced at him too, and also with hatred and anger. She had her own daydreams, her own plans, her own reflections; she understood perfectly well what her husband's dreams were. She knew who would be the first to try to grab her winnings. 75

"It's very nice making daydreams at other people's expense!" is what her eyes expressed. "No, don't you dare!"

Her husband understood her look; and in order to annoy his wife he glanced quickly, to spite her, at the fourth page on the newspaper and read out triumphantly: 80

"Series 9,499, number 46! Not 26!"

Hatred and hope both disappeared at once, and it immediately began to seem to Ivan Dmitritch and his wife that their rooms were dark and small and low-pitched, that the supper they had been eating was not doing them good, but lying heavy on their stomachs, that the evenings were long and wearisome. 85

126. The main conflict in this passage can best be described as Ivan's

  (A) believing his wife will not give him any money if she has won the lottery.
  (B) waiting to see whether his wife won the lottery.
  (C) wanting to go abroad in the autumn because the weather isn't very good then.
  (D) wanting to buy an estate when his wife doesn't want to.

127. When the author says that Ivan "gave a broad, senseless smile, like a baby when a bright object is shown it" (lines 26–27), he means that Ivan was

  (A) reacting to something instinctually.
  (B) happy about the prospect of winning the lottery.
  (C) unaware of how the lottery works.
  (D) very much in love with his wife.

128. The point of view from which the passage is told can best be described as that of

  (A) a narrator who has been in the position of almost winning the lottery.
  (B) a narrator who has a good grasp of human nature.
  (C) a friend of Ivan and his wife who hoped that the couple would win the lottery.
  (D) a person who had just met Ivan and his wife.

129. The image of "autumn with its rains and its cold evenings" (line 51)
suggests that Ivan

    (A) is fascinated by that season.
    (B) finds that season troublesome.
    (C) likes to walk in the rain.
    (D) wishes it were autumn.

130. Based on the information in the passage, if the lottery ticket is a winner,

    (A) Masha wants to give the money to her husband.
    (B) Ivan wants to buy a house and put money away.
    (C) Ivan wants to buy his wife fine clothing.
    (D) Masha would leave her husband.

131. It can reasonably be inferred that the author contrasts how Ivan thinks his
wife looks as opposed to how he thinks he looks to show that

    (A) his wife is no longer in love with him.
    (B) his wife has worked harder than he has.
    (C) he has an unrealistic picture of himself.
    (D) he is much younger than his wife.

132. It can reasonably be inferred that Ivan imagines that his wife

    (A) prefers not to win the money.
    (B) will take all the money and leave him nothing.
    (C) will share the money with him happily.
    (D) wants to go abroad to buy him new clothes.

133. Masha mirrors her husband's feelings by showing that she

    (A) has daydreams of her own.
    (B) has difficulty with the weather too.
    (C) wants them to stay at home.
    (D) is also sensitive to criticism.

134. What does the author mean when he has Ivan say, "She would begrudge
me every farthing" (line 67)?

    (A) Masha no longer thought Ivan was competent when it came to
          money.
    (B) Masha would be cautious when it came to buying things.
    (C) Masha was good with budgets and liked to keep track of their money.
    (D) Masha would be stingy with her money once she won the lottery.

135. Based on the information in the passage, what is the most likely reason Ivan wanted to wait before looking to see if they had the winning number?

(A) He hoped he was not the winner.
(B) He did not want his wife to be disappointed.
(C) He wanted to tease his wife.
(D) He wanted to savor the feeling of not knowing.

136. It may reasonably be inferred that Ivan and his wife both

(A) have strong fantasy worlds.
(B) want to give the money away.
(C) are extremely generous.
(D) want to tear up the lottery ticket.

137. At the end of the passage, what is the relevance of the author's saying that the rooms of their home seemed "dark and small and low-pitched" (lines 83–84)?

(A) It shows that they finally appreciate their lives.
(B) It suggests that they are no longer interested in winning the lottery.
(C) It shows that they are living in a terrible place.
(D) It suggests how their perception about their lives has changed.

138. The theme of the passage is best described as

(A) money can help cement a relationship.
(B) husbands are less aware of things than wives are.
(C) life without imagination is not worth living.
(D) greed can bring out the worst in people.

Social Sciences

Direct Election of the President

This passage is based on testimony before the U.S. Senate in 1997 by Becky Cain, then-president of the League of Women Voters. Her organization wanted to abolish the electoral college vote and have the presidential election determined by popular vote.

I am pleased to be here today to express the League's support for a constitutional amendment to abolish the Electoral College and establish the direct election of the President and Vice President of the United States by popular vote of the American people.

Since 1970, the League has supported an amendment to the Constitution that would abolish the Electoral College and establish a direct, popular vote for the President and Vice President of the United States. . . . Our method of electing a President must be changed to ensure a more representative government.

Political developments since the 1970s have only underscored the need for the elimination of the Electoral College system. The downward trend in voter partici- 10 pation, coupled with increased cynicism and skepticism amongst the public about the ability of elected leaders to provide meaningful representation, are the warning signs of a potential electoral fiasco.

Picture if you will a future national election in which a presidential candidate receives a majority of the popular vote, but is denied the 270 votes necessary for 15 election by the Electoral College. This has already happened once in our nation's history, when, in 1888, Grover Cleveland outpolled Benjamin Harrison in the popular vote but lost the Electoral College vote by 233 to 168. It caused a public furor then, when political office was often gained through backroom deals and closed-door maneuvering. Imagine the public outcry today, after a long primary 20 campaign and a grueling race for the Presidency. Imagine the public's rage at being denied their candidate of choice.

Now go one step further. Consider a close three-way race for President in which no candidate earns the necessary Electoral College votes to win. This has happened twice before in our nation's history, in 1801 and 1825, when the House 25 of Representatives chose Thomas Jefferson and John Quincy Adams, respectively. While the League believes both of these men were great presidents, we are troubled about the potential for a future presidential candidate with the highest number of popular votes to lose the election in a House of Representatives dominated by one or another political party. 30

In the twentieth century, we have only narrowly avoided a series of constitutional crises in which the Electoral College could have overruled the popular vote.

In the 1916 presidential election, a shift of only 2,000 votes in California would have given Charles Evans Hughes the necessary electoral votes to defeat Woodrow Wilson, despite Wilson's half-million-vote nationwide plurality. 35

In 1948, a shift of only 30,000 votes in three states would have delivered the White House to Governor Dewey, in spite of the fact that he trailed President Truman by some 2.1 million popular votes.

In 1960, a shift of only 13,000 votes in five states would have made Richard Nixon president. 40

In 1968, a shift of 42,000 votes in three states would have denied Nixon an Electoral College victory and thrown the election into the House of Representatives.

In 1976, a shift of only 9,300 votes would have elected Gerald Ford, even though he trailed Jimmy Carter in the popular vote by 1.6 million ballots. . . .

In a nation where voting rights are grounded in the one-person, one-vote 45 principle, the Electoral College is a hopeless anachronism.

The current system is unfair for two reasons.

First, a citizen's individual vote has more weight if he or she lives in a state with a small population than if that citizen lives in a state with a large population. . . .

The system is also unfair because a citizen's individual vote has more weight if 50 the percentage of voter participation in the state is low. . . .

Moreover, the electoral vote does not reflect the volume of voter participation within a state. If only a few voters go to the polls, all the electoral votes of the state are still cast.

Finally, the Electoral College system is flawed because the Constitution does 55 not bind presidential electors to vote for the candidates to whom they have been pledged. For example, in 1948, 1960, and 1976, individual electors pledged to the top two vote-getters cast their votes for third-place finishers and also-rans.

Defecting electors in a close race could cause a crisis of confidence in our electoral system. 60

For all these reasons, the League believes that the presidential election method should incorporate the one-person, one-vote principle. The President should be directly elected by the people he or she will represent, just as the other federally elected officials are in this country. Direct election is the most representative system. It is the only system that guarantees the President will have received the most 65 popular votes. It also encourages voter participation by giving voters a direct and equal role in the election of the President.

When the Constitution was first written, our nation was a vastly different kind of democracy than it is today. Only white, male property owners could vote. The 15th Amendment gave black men the right to vote. The 19th Amendment gave 70 women the vote. The 26th Amendment established the right of citizens 18 years of age and older to vote.

The time has come to take the next step to ensure a broad-based, representative democracy. Fairness argues for it. Retaining the fragile faith of American voters in our representative system demands it. We urge the House and the Senate to pass a 75 constitutional amendment abolishing the Electoral College system and establishing the direct popular election of our President and Vice President.

139. When Cain says that political developments have "underscored the need for the elimination of the Electoral College system" (lines 9–10), she means that these developments have

(A) denied the need for elimination of the Electoral College system.
(B) ignored the need for elimination of the Electoral College system.
(C) emphasized the need for elimination of the Electoral College system.
(D) forgotten the need for elimination of the Electoral College system.

140. Which of the following statements best describes what happens when no candidate in a three-way race for president gets enough Electoral College votes to win?

(A) The Senate decides between the candidates with the largest number of electoral votes.
(B) The election is decided by the popular vote.
(C) The candidate with the least amount of electoral votes must give up his or her votes to the candidates with the most electoral votes.
(D) The House of Representatives decides who will be president.

141. Which of the following statements best expresses the main point of the passage?

(A) The Electoral College system is flawed and should be changed.

(B) Electors do not have to vote for candidates to whom they have been pledged.

(C) The 26th Amendment established the right of citizens 18 years of age and older to vote.

(D) Fewer people are voting today because they feel out of touch with government.

142. When the author says that "the Constitution does not bind presidential electors to vote for the candidates to whom they have been pledged" (lines 55–57), she means that

(A) no one can predict who will win a particular state's electors.

(B) people have control over whom electors will vote for.

(C) electors do not have to vote for the candidate that voters picked.

(D) elections are often determined by the electors and not the people.

143. Based on the information in the passage, in a presidential election, what happens to a person's vote for Candidate A if Candidate B carries the state?

(A) It is not counted.

(B) It becomes a vote for Candidate B.

(C) The vote is recorded under protest.

(D) The person has a chance to vote in another state.

144. When the author calls the Electoral College "a hopeless anachronism" (line 46), she means that the Electoral College is

(A) not large enough.

(B) outdated.

(C) voted into office.

(D) not strong enough.

145. Which of the following positions is supported by the statement that "the 19th Amendment gave women the vote" (lines 70–71)?

(A) A citizen's individual vote has more weight if he or she lives in a state with a small population.

(B) Political office has been gained through backroom deals.

(C) The Constitution has been updated.

(D) The president should be directly elected by the people.

146. According to the author, all of the following are reasons for abandoning the Electoral College system EXCEPT

(A) the problem that could arise if there is a three-way race.
(B) the possibility that the Electoral College could overrule the popular vote.
(C) the problem of some votes having more weight than others.
(D) the idea that popular votes should be made more significant.

147. When Cain refers to "defecting electors" who did not cast their votes for the winners in their states' elections, she means that the electors

(A) feared following the voters' choice.
(B) abandoned their responsibility.
(C) were less than perfect.
(D) gave up too easily.

148. When the author says that "retaining the fragile faith of American voters in our representative system" (lines 74–75) demands changing the electoral system, she seems to suggest that the voters are

(A) committed to our present form of democracy.
(B) losing trust in the way that they are represented.
(C) not interested in the democratic process.
(D) more inclined to vote for new candidates.

149. It can reasonably be inferred that the author would most likely support

(A) reviewing all procedures to see if they need updating.
(B) having senators decide who the president will be.
(C) having presidents appointed by the House of Representatives.
(D) giving more power to the Electoral College.

150. In the last paragraph, the author makes it clear that the amendment should be passed because

(A) people would be more likely to vote for newcomers as presidents.
(B) people would ultimately choose more capable presidents.
(C) presidential elections would most likely be run in an orderly fashion.
(D) voters would take more interest in the process of electing a president.

151. It can reasonably be inferred that the author mentions the presidential race between Gerald Ford and Jimmy Carter in order to

(A) emphasize the lack of consistency in the electoral process for choosing a president.
(B) explain why Carter won the presidential race.
(C) discuss the values of each candidate.
(D) show how little it would have taken to change who won the presidency.

152. Based on the information in the passage, the purpose of the author is to

    (A) explain why the Electoral College system should be abandoned.
    (B) explain how the president is voted into office.
    (C) instruct on the proper method of casting electoral votes.
    (D) tell how many electoral votes are needed to become president.

Paired Passages: Humanities

Passage 1: *Indian Boyhood* by Charles A. Eastman

This excerpt is adapted from the memoir of Charles A. Eastman (1858–1939), named Hakadah at birth and later named Ohiyesa. Part Native American and part Anglo-American, Eastman was a doctor, writer, and activist who accomplished a great deal for Native Americans. He is considered the first person to write about U.S. history from a Native American perspective.

With the first March thaw the thoughts of the Indian women of my childhood days turned promptly to the annual sugarmaking. This industry was chiefly followed by the old men and women and the children. The rest of the tribe went out upon the spring fur-hunt at this season, leaving us at home to make the sugar.

My grandmother worked like a beaver in these days (or rather like a muskrat,   5 as the Indians say; for this industrious little animal sometimes collects as many as six or eight bushels of edible roots for the winter, only to be robbed of his store by some of our people). If there was prospect of a good sugaring season, she now made a second and even a third canoe to contain the sap.

My grandmother did not confine herself to canoe-making. She also collected a good   10 supply of fuel for the fires, for she would not have much time to gather wood when the sap began to flow. Presently the weather moderated and the snow began to melt. Now the women began to test the trees—moving leisurely among them, axe in hand, and striking a single quick blow, to see if the sap would appear. The trees, like people, have their individual characters; some were ready to yield up their life-blood, while others   15 were more reluctant. Now one of the birchen basins was set under each tree, and a hardwood chip driven deep into the cut which the axe had made. From the corners of this chip—at first drop by drop, then more freely—the sap trickled into the little dishes.

A long fire was now made in the sugar house, and a row of brass kettles suspended over the blaze. The sap was collected by the women in tin or birchen buck-   20 ets and poured into the canoes, from which the kettles were kept filled. Each boy claimed one kettle for his especial charge. It was his duty to see that the fire was kept up under it, to watch lest it boil over, and finally, when the sap became syrup, to test it upon the snow, dipping it out with a wooden paddle. So frequent were these tests that for the first day or two we consumed nearly all that could be made;   25 and it was not until the sweetness began to pall that my grandmother set herself in earnest to store up sugar for future use. She made it into cakes of various forms, in birchen molds, and sometimes in hollow canes or reeds, and the bills of ducks and geese. Being a prudent woman, she did not give it to us after the first month or so, except upon special occasions, and it was thus made to last almost the year around.   30

Passage 2: "Remarks Concerning the Savages of North America" by Benjamin Franklin

Adapted from Benjamin Franklin's essay, this excerpt contrasts Native American (here referred to as Indian) customs with the customs of colonial Americans. It highlights the absurdity of criticizing another's culture simply because it does not mirror one's own.

Savages we call them, because their Manners differ from ours, which we think the Perfection of Civility. They think the same of theirs. Perhaps if we could examine the Manners of different Nations with Impartiality, we should find no People so rude as to be without Rules of Politeness, nor any so polite as not to have some Remains of Rudeness. 5

The Indian Men when young are Hunters and Warriors; when old, Counsellors; for all their Government is by Counsel of the Sages; there is no Force, there are no Prisons, no Officers to compel Obedience, or inflict Punishment. The Indian Women till the Ground, dress the Food, nurse and bring up the Children, & preserve & hand down to Posterity the Memory of public Transactions. These Employments of 10 Men and Women are accounted natural & honorable, Having few artificial Wants, they have abundance of Leisure for Improvement by Conversation. Our laborious Manner of Life compar'd with theirs, they esteem slavish & base; and the Learning on which we value ourselves, they regard as frivolous & useless.

An Instance of this occurr'd at the Treaty of Lancaster in Pensilvania, anno 1744, 15 between the Government of Virginia and the Six Nations. The Commissioners from Virginia acquainted the Indians by a Speech, that there was at Williamsburg a College, with a Fund for Educating Indian youth; and that if the Six Nations would send down half a dozen of their young Lads to that College, the Government would take Care that they should be well provided for, and instructed in all the Learning of the White 20 People. It is one of the Indian Rules of Politeness not to answer a public Proposition the same day that it is made; they think it would be treating it as a light matter. They therefore deferr'd their Answer till the Day following; when their Speaker began by expressing their deep Sense of the Kindness of the Virginia Government in making them that Offer, for we know, says he, that you highly esteem the kind of Learning taught in those 25 Colleges, and that the Maintenance of our young Men while with you, would be very expensive to you. We are convinc'd therefore that you mean to do us Good by your Proposal, and we thank you heartily. But we have had some Experience with your kind of education: Several of our young People were formerly brought up at the Colleges of the Northern Provinces; they were instructed in all your Sciences; but when they came back 30 to us they were bad Runners ignorant of every means of living in the Woods, unable to bear either Cold or Hunger, knew neither how to build a Cabin, take a Deer or kill an Enemy, spoke our Language imperfectly, were therefore neither fit for Hunters Warriors, or Counsellors. They were totally good for nothing. We are however not the less oblig'd by your kind Offer tho' we decline accepting it; and to show our grateful Sense of it, if 35 the Gentlemen of Virginia will send us a Dozen of their Sons, we will take great Care of their Education, instruct them in all we know, and make Men of them.

Passage 1 Questions

153. When the author says, "Now the women began to test the trees . . . axe in hand, and striking a single quick blow, to see if the sap would appear" (lines 12–14), the author means that the women were

(A) making canoes from the trees.
(B) gathering wood for the fires.
(C) checking to see if the trees should be tapped.
(D) getting ready to make the fires.

154. The grandmother can best be described as

(A) austere and cold.
(B) diligent and productive.
(C) lenient and forgiving.
(D) moral and demanding.

155. Based on the passage, what feelings did Eastman have toward his grandmother?

(A) He thought she worked too hard.
(B) He wanted to help her more.
(C) He admired her strength.
(D) He worried she might hurt herself.

156. It can reasonably be inferred that the grandmother

(A) would have preferred not participating in the sugar gathering.
(B) did not want her grandson working so hard.
(C) felt she needed more important work to do.
(D) was in charge of the maple sugar project.

157. Which of the following statements best describes the author's attitude toward his childhood?

(A) He has warm feelings about his childhood.
(B) He feels that it was a difficult time for him.
(C) He wonders if his past was a bad influence on him.
(D) He thinks that his past presented many challenges that were beyond him.

Passage 2 Questions

158. The main point of the passage is

(A) that Indians should not be judged harshly for not understanding colonial culture.
(B) that "civilized" and "savage" are subjective concepts.
(C) to relay some of the customs of the Indians at that time.
(D) that a "good" education depends on what is meant by "school."

159. In which way did the Indians govern their people?

(A) By threat from warriors

(B) By harsh punishments including shunning

(C) By a group of elders

(D) Through rules and regulations

160. The Indian people considered the colonials' lifestyle to be

(A) arduous.

(B) luxurious.

(C) interesting.

(D) pointless.

161. All of these skills were considered an important part of the education of the young Indian man EXCEPT

(A) fluent speaking.

(B) expert hunting and fighting.

(C) endurance running.

(D) smoking meats.

162. From the passage, it could be reasonably inferred that

(A) the Indian elders thought that white colleges would be a detriment to their children.

(B) the Indians were offended by the colonials' offer to educate their young men.

(C) the colonials wanted to exchange children in order to learn about each other's cultures.

(D) It was important to the Indians that their children have an opportunity to experience the white culture.

Paired Passage Questions

163. Which is the best comparison of the tones of the two passages?

(A) Passage 1 is nostalgic while Passage 2 is slightly ironic.

(B) Passage 1 is impersonal while Passage 2 is argumentative.

(C) Both passages have a humorous tone.

(D) Passage 1 is objective while Passage 2 is sarcastic.

164. In contrast to Passage 2, the author of Passage 1 uses

(A) hyperbole to make his point.

(B) examples to illustrate his point.

(C) metaphors and similes to illustrate his story.

(D) alliteration to create a mood.

165. How would the author of Passage 1 most likely respond to this sentence from Passage 2: "Having few artificial Wants, they have abundance of Leisure for Improvement by Conversation."

(A) The life of the Indian was much more relaxed and simple than that of a colonial.

(B) Actually, the Indians did not spend much time in conversation; they were a quiet people.

(C) Indian men may have had plenty of time for leisure, but Indian women worked long and hard days.

(D) As in every society, some people worked hard and some people loafed.

166. Which is the best comparison of the portrayal of Indian life in Passage 1 and Passage 2?

(A) Simple compared to complicated.

(B) Without structure compared to organized.

(C) Hardworking compared to relaxed.

(D) Rustic compared to advanced.

Natural Sciences

Effects of Blue Light

With the advent of so many electronic devices, this passage on blue light is extremely timely. Perhaps in the future, more effort will be made to control this form of light.

Blue light is the light emitted from TV screens and computer monitors. It is also emitted from the backlit, luminous screens of tablet computers and iPads, e-readers, and smartphones, as well as from energy-saving fluorescent lights. As the number of electronic devices has increased exponentially in recent years, there has been a considerable amount of research conducted on what effect, if   5 any, increased exposure to blue light has on humans. There is also an increased concern, because these devices are held much closer to the eye than a TV screen, or even a computer monitor.

Light consists of electromagnetic particles that move in waves. Radio waves have the longest wavelength, and gamma rays have the shortest. Visible light, which   10 can be discerned by the human eye, makes up only a very small part of the entire electromagnetic spectrum, ranging from red with the longest wavelength to violet with the shortest. Blue light has a wavelength of about 450 to 500 nanometers. A nanometer is equivalent to one billionth of a meter.

Researchers at the University of Basel in Switzerland recently studied the effects   15 of evening use of computer monitors with light-emitting diode (LED)–backlit screens that emitted blue light. Thirteen male volunteers were studied in a controlled setting, where they were exposed to five hours of computer light in the evening and nighttime hours. Some used blue light LED monitors; others used white, non-LED–backlit screens. Compared to the volunteers using white screens, those exposed to blue light showed a significant, measurable decrease in cognitive performance, attention span, and alertness. Most importantly, the results showed a significant inhibition of the normal nighttime rise of endogenous (built-in) melatonin in the blue-light user group.

Melatonin is a hormone secreted by the pineal gland, located in the forebrain. It is how the body regulates what is defined as circadian timing, an approximately 24-hour cycle that both animals and plants are governed by. The word *circadian* comes from the Latin words *circa* ("around") and *dies* ("day"). Melatonin is released when it grows dark; during daylight hours, the hormone is not released. The hormone therefore is utilized to regulate daily sleep/wake cycles; light is the factor that synchronizes the circadian system. According to the National Sleep Foundation, studies have linked a host of illnesses, ranging from depression, obesity, diabetes, and cardiovascular disease to poor sleeping habits. In addition, not getting enough sleep can cause irritability, and even anger or rage.

Engineers at Rensselaer Polytechnic Institute (RPI) in Troy, New York, conducted a thorough study of the effects of blue light from self-luminous, backlit electronic devices at the Lighting Research Center. Adolescents and young adults were given tablet computers, which they used for reading, playing games, and watching movies during the evening hours.

The participants were divided into three groups. The first group wore no glasses, the second (the control group) wore clear goggles fitted with blue-light LEDs, and the third group wore orange-tinted goggles. The orange tint filters out shorter-wavelength light. Each of the participants wore a dimesimeter, a datalogging device developed at RPI that records light levels for up to a month; it is very portable—about the size of a dime.

The three groups were monitored and had their melatonin levels measured. The findings built on what the Basel researchers discovered: extensive use of these devices interferes with the body's normal nighttime increase in the release of endogenous melatonin. The group with the orange glasses had the least suppression of melatonin, those with no glasses fell in the middle range, and those with the LED goggles had the greatest suppression of melatonin. In fact, using these devices two hours before retiring lowered melatonin levels by 22% in the control group. It is precisely this age bracket, adolescents and young adults, who are most prone to sleep disruption and the consequent pattern of behavior changes. The task being performed on the device, as well as its distance from the retina, affected the level of melatonin suppression by as much as a factor of 10.

The engineers at RPI hope that the results of the study will encourage manufacturers to develop circadian-friendly electronic devices, which would reduce circadian stimulation in nighttime use for a better night's sleep and increase circadian stimulation during daytime use for more alertness. A software engineer has developed a program, called f.lux, that decreases the blue light emanating from a screen; screen color is adjusted automatically. To use the software, which can be downloaded for free, the user simply enters his longitude and latitude. This program is a step in the right direction for night owls who stare at a screen late at night.

167. The word *spectrum*, as used in the second paragraph (line 12), most nearly means

(A) distribution of energy.
(B) collection of molecules.
(C) social association.
(D) saline solution.

168. According to the passage, visible light

(A) has a wavelength of 450 to 500 nanometers.
(B) is not detected by the human eye.
(C) travels in waves.
(D) has the shortest wavelength.

169. The main point of the third paragraph (lines 15–24) is that

(A) blue light is emitted from LED screens.
(B) the research in Basel was conducted in a controlled setting.
(C) exposure to blue light can have physical and mental side effects.
(D) endogenous melatonin is increased after five hours of computer use.

170. The phrase *cognitive performance*, as used in the third paragraph (lines 15–24), most nearly means

(A) state of ignorance.
(B) mental process.
(C) personality trait.
(D) successful conclusion.

171. When the author states that the number of handheld electronic devices has "increased exponentially" (line 4), the author is most likely concerned that

(A) the deleterious effects of blue-light exposure are greater because the devices are held closer.
(B) it is another sign that young people spend too much time texting on their smartphones.
(C) manufacturers will not develop circadian-friendly electronic devices.
(D) adolescents don't read books before they go to bed like they used to.

172. The main point of the fourth paragraph (lines 25–34) is that

(A) circadian timing is an approximately 24-hour cycle.
(B) melatonin governs daily cycles of sleeping and waking.
(C) melatonin is released when night falls.
(D) the pineal gland is located in the forebrain.

173. According to the passage, researchers in both Basel, Switzerland, and Troy, New York, noticed that

(A) a host of illnesses can be linked to poor sleeping habits.
(B) the pineal gland is responsible for the secretion of melatonin.
(C) there is a computer program called f.lux that decreases blue light.
(D) using computers at night measurably lowers melatonin levels.

174. The author of the passage would most likely recommend all of the following actions to reduce the melatonin-lowering effects of blue light EXCEPT

(A) watching movies on TV rather than on a tablet.
(B) cutting down on nighttime computer use.
(C) wearing a dimesimeter while using the computer.
(D) using the software known as f.lux.

175. When the author states that "studies have linked a host of illnesses, ranging from depression, obesity, diabetes, and cardiovascular disease to poor sleeping habits" (lines 32–33), the author is most likely suggesting that readers

(A) add a melatonin supplement to their diet.
(B) try to get as much sleep as they can.
(C) replace their energy-efficient fluorescent lighting.
(D) be cognizant of this link when using a computer a lot at night.

176. The main point of the seventh paragraph (lines 46–56) is that

(A) adolescents and young adults are prone to sleep problems.
(B) it is a good idea to wear orange-tinted goggles.
(C) the Basel and RPI research yielded similar results.
(D) an electronic device should be held as far as possible from the eyes.

177. When the author says that f.lux software is "a step in the right direction" (lines 63–64), it can reasonably be inferred that the author

(A) feels that not enough research is being done by scientists on blue light.
(B) thinks electronic devices should have f.lux software already installed.
(C) wants parents to make sure their children download the f.lux software.
(D) is hopeful about new ways of controlling blue light.

178. According to the passage, all of the following statements are true about blue light EXCEPT that

   (A) it has the shortest wavelength of all light.

   (B) it cannot be seen by the human eye.

   (C) its rays interfere with the production of melatonin.

   (D) it is used in most electronic devices.

179. The last paragraph of the passage suggests that the RPI engineers

   (A) believe manufacturers are working on devices that reduce circadian stimulation.

   (B) feel that their study offers useful information to computer users.

   (C) hope that computer users discontinue excessive nighttime use.

   (D) will continue their research into the effects of blue-light emission.

180. Which of the following statements is the main point of the passage?

   (A) There is a growing body of evidence that users of handheld electronic devices should use them with caution, especially at night.

   (B) Melatonin plays an important role in regulating the body's response to getting the proper amount of sleep.

   (C) Adolescents and young adults should not hold handheld electronic devices too close to their eyes.

   (D) If you are going to use a handheld electronic device for a long period of time, download and install f.lux software.

Prose Fiction

"The Mouse" by Saki

H. H. Munro (1870–1916), whose pen name was Saki, wrote many short stories about unusual subjects and with comic twists. This passage, adapted from Saki's short story "The Mouse," is no exception.

    Theodoric Voler had been brought up by a fond mother, whose chief concern had been to keep him away from what she called the coarser realities of life. To a man of his temperament and upbringing, even a simple railway journey was crammed with petty annoyances and minor discords. As he settled himself down in a second-class compartment one September morning, he was aware of   5 ruffled feelings and general mental discomfort.

    He had been staying at a country vicarage with friends. The pony carriage that was to take him to the station had never been properly ordered. When the moment for his departure drew near, Theodoric found himself obliged to ask the vicar's daughter for help with harnessing the pony. That meant groping about in   10 an ill-lighted outbuilding called a stable that smelled very like one—except where it smelled of mice.

As the train glided out of the station, Theodoric's nervous imagination brought up the image of a strange stable yard odor escaping from him. Fortunately, the only other occupant of the compartment, a lady of about the same age as himself, was sleeping. The train was not due to stop till the terminal was reached, in about an hour's time. And yet the train had scarcely attained its normal speed before he became aware that he was not alone with the slumbering lady. He was not even alone in his own clothes.

A warm, creeping movement over his flesh betrayed the unwelcome presence of a stray mouse, which had evidently dashed into his clothes while he was in the stable. Stamps and shakes and pinches failed to get rid of the mouse, and the lawful occupant of the clothes lay back against the cushions and endeavored rapidly to evolve some means for putting an end to the dual ownership. Nothing less drastic than partial undressing would ease him of his tormentor. But to undress in the presence of a lady was an idea that made his eartips tingle in a blush of shame. The mouse kept climbing up his leg, and then it would lose its footing and slip for half an inch or so. And then, in fright, or more probably temper, it bit. Theodoric was forced to undertake the most bold undertaking of his life. Keeping an agonized watch on his slumbering fellow traveler, he swiftly and noiselessly put the ends of his railway rug on the racks on either side of the carriage.

In the narrow dressing room that he had thus improvised he proceeded to get himself partially and the mouse entirely from the pant leg. As the mouse gave a wild leap to the floor, the rug slipped down and the noise woke the sleeper. With a movement almost quicker than the mouse's, Theodoric jumped on the rug and hauled it chin-high over himself. The blood raced and beat in the veins of his neck and forehead, while he waited dumbly for the communication cord to be pulled. The lady, however, contented herself with a silent stare at her strangely muffled companion. How much had she seen, Theodoric queried to himself; and in any case, what on earth must she think of his present posture? The lady, however, just sat back and stared at him.

"I think I have caught a chill," he said to her desperately.

"Really, I'm sorry," she replied. "I was just going to ask you if you would open this window."

"I think it's malaria," he added, his teeth chattering slightly, as much from fright as from a desire to support his theory.

"I suppose you caught it in the tropics?"

Theodoric, whose acquaintance with the tropics was limited to an annual present of a chest of tea from an uncle in Ceylon, felt that even the malaria was slipping from him. Would it be possible, he wondered, to explain the real state of affairs to her?

"Are you afraid of mice?" he ventured, growing, if possible, more scarlet in the face.

"Not unless they came in quantities. Why do you ask?"

"I had one crawling inside my clothes just now," said Theodoric in a voice that hardly seemed his own. "It was a most awkward situation."

"It must have been, if you wear your clothes at all tight," she observed. "But mice have strange ideas of comfort."

"I had to get rid of it while you were asleep," he continued. Then, with a gulp, he added, "It was getting rid of it that brought me to—to this." 60

"Surely getting rid of one small mouse wouldn't bring on a chill," she exclaimed, with a lightheartedness that Theodoric thought abominable.

Evidently she had realized a bit of his predicament and was enjoying his confusion. With every minute that passed, the train was rushing nearer to the terminal. There, dozens of eyes would be watching him instead of just the eyes in the corner 65 of the carriage. There was only one chance. That was the hope that his fellow traveler might fall back asleep. But as the minutes passed by, that chance ebbed away. The glance which Theodoric gave her from time to time showed that she was still awake.

"I think we must be getting near now," she commented. 70

Theodoric had already noticed with growing terror the small, ugly dwellings passing by. They were almost there. Like a hunted beast breaking cover, he threw aside his rug, and struggled into his disheveled clothes. Then, as he sank back in his seat, clothed and almost delirious, the train slowed down to a final crawl, and the woman spoke. 75

"Would you be so kind," she asked, "as to get me a porter to put me into a cab? It's a shame to trouble you when you're feeling unwell, but being blind makes one so helpless at a railway station."

181. It can reasonably be inferred that Theodoric

    (A) travels a good deal.

    (B) was an only child.

    (C) was protected as a child.

    (D) enjoys meeting new people.

182. Which of the following statements best describes the theme of the passage?

    (A) People learn from their mistakes.

    (B) Traveling allows for new adventures.

    (C) Things are not always as they appear.

    (D) People are apt to do odd things when traveling.

183. The event that most significantly affects the outcome of the story is

    (A) the disclosure that the companion is blind.

    (B) the rug falling to the floor.

    (C) Theodoric's removing his clothes.

    (D) Theodoric's being bitten by the mouse.

184. It can reasonably be inferred that the reason Theodoric tells his traveling companion he has malaria (line 45) is to

(A) amuse himself during the long trip.
(B) show that he knows a lot about the tropics.
(C) make it appear that he had lived in the tropics.
(D) make up an excuse for being wrapped up in a rug.

185. What is the most likely reason that Theodoric decided to put his clothes back on?

(A) He realized the rug looked silly on him.
(B) He thought the conductor would be coming shortly.
(C) He realized he would have to get off the train in a little while.
(D) He thought he should straighten up for the sake of his companion.

186. The situation with the mouse caused Theodoric to become

(A) more observant than he was before.
(B) more forgiving than he was before.
(C) more reasonable than he was before.
(D) more daring than he was before.

187. When the author says that "the lawful occupant of the clothes lay back against the cushions and endeavored rapidly to evolve some means for putting an end to the dual ownership" (lines 22–24), he means that

(A) the mouse was nesting in Theodoric's clothes.
(B) Theodoric's clothes were borrowed.
(C) Theodoric's clothes were old.
(D) the mouse was inside Theodoric's clothes.

188. Based on the information in the sixth paragraph (line 42), Theodoric tells his traveling companion that he has a chill in order to

(A) suggest that it is cold on the train.
(B) explain why he is covered by a rug.
(C) suggest that he needs her help.
(D) explain why he is fully clothed.

189. Which of the following statements best describes the author's perspective on Theodoric in the story?

(A) He finds Theodoric humorous.
(B) He thinks Theodoric is overly cynical.
(C) He believes that Theodoric has a great deal of potential.
(D) He worries that Theodoric may suffer physically because of his nerves.

190. In the fifth paragraph (lines 32–41), why does Theodoric think that his traveling companion will pull the communication cord?

(A) He thinks that she wants to order some food.
(B) He is worried that she has seen him without his clothes.
(C) He knows that she is blind and is seeking help.
(D) He wants her to call for help.

191. Based on the information in the seventeenth paragraph (lines 63–69), what does Theodoric think of his traveling companion?

(A) He believes that she is not well.
(B) He thinks she is making fun of him.
(C) He thinks that she may be odd.
(D) He believes that she wants him to be friendlier.

192. It can reasonably be inferred that the author waits until the end of the story to reveal that the traveling companion is blind because the author

(A) does not think it is an important detail.
(B) does not want to upset the reader earlier.
(C) wants to surprise the reader with the information.
(D) wants to make the reader feel compassion for the companion.

193. The tone of the passage is best described as

(A) bitter and acrid.
(B) sarcastic.
(C) tongue-in-cheek.
(D) whimsical.

194. The probable effect that the words of his traveling companion had on Theodoric was that he felt

(A) betrayed.
(B) relieved.
(C) angered.
(D) troubled.

CHAPTER **4**

Set 4 Reading Questions

Prose Fiction

"The Last Class—the Story of a Little Alsatian" by Alphonse Daudet

This passage is adapted from a short story by Alphonse Daudet (1840–1897). It takes place in 1870, when Prussian forces under King Otto Bismarck attacked France. As a result, the French districts of Alsace and Lorraine, which bordered Prussia (modern Germany), came under Prussian rule.

I was very late for school that morning, and I was terribly afraid of being scolded, especially as Monsieur Hamel had told us that he should examine us on participles, and I did not know the first thing about them. For a moment I thought of staying away from school and wandering about the fields. I could hear the blackbirds whistling on the edge of the 5 wood, and in the field, behind the sawmill, the Prussians going through their drill. All that was much more tempting to me than the rules concerning participles; but I had the strength to resist, and I ran as fast as I could to school.

Usually, at the beginning of school, there was a great uproar which 10 could be heard in the street, desks opening and closing, lessons repeated aloud in unison, with our ears stuffed in order to learn quicker, and the teacher's stout ruler beating on the desk.

I counted on all this noise to reach my bench unnoticed; but as it happened, that day everything was quiet, like a Sunday morning. I had to 15 open the door and enter, in the midst of that perfect silence.

Monsieur Hamel looked at me with no sign of anger and said very gently:

"Go at once to your seat, my little Frantz; we were going to begin without you." 20

I stepped over the bench and sat down at once at my desk. Not until then, when I had partly recovered from my fright, did I notice that our teacher had on his handsome blue coat, which he wore only on days of inspection or of distribution of prizes. Moreover, there was something extraordinary, something solemn about the whole class. But what surprised me most was to see at the back of the room, on the benches which were usually empty, some people from the village sitting, as silent as we were. They all seemed depressed. 25

While I was wondering at all this, Monsieur Hamel had mounted his platform, and in the same gentle and serious voice with which he had welcomed me, he said to us: 30

"My children, this is the last time that I shall teach you. Orders have come from Berlin to teach nothing but German in the schools of Alsace and Lorraine. The new teacher arrives tomorrow. This is the last class in French, so I beg you to be very attentive."

Those few words overwhelmed me. My last class in French! 35

And I barely knew how to write! So I should never learn! How angry I was with myself because of the time I had wasted, the lessons I had missed! And it was the same about Monsieur Hamel. The thought that he was going away, that I should never see him again, made me forget the punishments, the blows with the ruler.

I was at that point in my reflections, when I heard my name called. What 40 would I not have given to be able to say from beginning to end that famous rule about participles without a slip! But I got mixed up at the first words, and I stood there swaying against my bench, with a full heart, afraid to raise my head. I heard Monsieur Hamel speaking to me:

"I will not scold you, my little Frantz; you must be punished enough; that is 45 the way it goes; every day we say to ourselves: 'Pshaw! I have time enough. I will learn tomorrow.' And then you see what happens."

Then, passing from one thing to another, Monsieur Hamel began to talk to us about the French language, saying that it was the most beautiful language in the world; that we must always retain it among ourselves, and never forget it, because 50 when a people falls into servitude, "so long as it clings to its language, it is as if it held the key to its prison."

Then he took the grammar and read us our lesson. I was amazed to see how readily I understood. Everything that he said seemed so easy to me, so easy. I believed, too, that I had never listened so closely, and that he had never been 55 so patient with his explanations.

When the lesson was at an end, we passed to writing.

From time to time, when I raised my eyes from my paper, I saw Monsieur Hamel sitting motionless in his chair and staring at the objects about him as if he wished to carry away in his glance the whole of his little schoolhouse. Think of it! 60 For forty years he had been there in the same place, with his yard in front of him and his class just as it was! What a heart-rending thing it must have been for that poor man to leave all those things, and to hear his sister walking back and forth in the room overhead, packing their trunks! For they were to go away the next day—to leave the province forever. 65

However, he had the courage to keep the class to the end. After the writing, we had the lesson in history; then the little ones sang all together.

Suddenly the church clock struck twelve. At the same moment, the bugles of the Prussians returning from drill blared under our windows. Monsieur Hamel rose, pale as death, from his chair. Never had he seemed to me so tall. 70

"My friends," he said, "my friends, I—I—"

But he could not finish the sentence.

Thereupon he turned to the blackboard, took a piece of chalk, and wrote in the largest letters he could:

"VIVE LA FRANCE!"[1] 75

Then he stood there, with his head resting against the wall, and without speaking, he motioned to us with his hand:

"That is all; go."

195. The point of view from which the passage is told can best be described as that of

   (A) a narrator who is good at his studies, but not sensitive to the moment.
   (B) a narrator who realizes that his world will never be the same.
   (C) a friend of Monsieur Hamel who is transcribing what his last French class was like.
   (D) a person who was in the classroom observing, but who is new to the town.

196. When Frantz says, "but I had the strength to resist, and I ran as fast as I could to school" (lines 8–9), he means that he

   (A) wanted to get to school to help Monsieur Hamel.
   (B) was strong enough to be able to run to school.
   (C) resisted saying something to the Prussians.
   (D) overcame his desire to skip school.

197. It can reasonably be inferred that the villagers attended the class to

   (A) pay their respects to Monsieur Hamel.
   (B) decide whether Monsieur Hamel should be fired.
   (C) learn to speak French better.
   (D) find out how well the students were doing with their French.

198. When Frantz says, "there was something extraordinary, something solemn about the whole class" (lines 24–25), it can reasonably be inferred that Frantz

   (A) was upset about being late.
   (B) was worried about French grammar.
   (C) thought something bad was happening.
   (D) believed Monsieur Hamel's sister was sick.

---

[1] French for "Long live France!"

199. Based on the information in the passage, what effect did the villagers' presence in the class have on Frantz?

(A) It made Frantz think he was in trouble.
(B) It told Frantz that something odd was going on.
(C) It made Frantz even more nervous.
(D) It caused Frantz to forget his lesson.

200. From comments made by Frantz, it can be assumed that Monsieur Hamel's treatment of Frantz during the last class was

(A) more critical of Frantz than usual.
(B) more sympathetic than before.
(C) less interested in Frantz than before.
(D) less kindly than usual.

201. It can reasonably be inferred that when Frantz heard that this was the last French class, he was

(A) worried about learning German.
(B) sure that he would do better learning German than French.
(C) brokenhearted because Monsieur Hamel would be gone.
(D) relieved that he would no longer be punished by Monsieur Hamel.

202. The theme of the passage is that

(A) school teachers are emotional.
(B) young men should be more studious.
(C) some changes can be painful.
(D) life holds many joys.

203. Monsieur Hamel says that Frantz "must be punished enough" (line 45), because

(A) Frantz had been punished by Monsieur Hamel a great deal before.
(B) Monsieur Hamel feels that he was wrong to have punished Frantz.
(C) Frantz would not have the chance to study French again.
(D) Monsieur Hamel thinks Frantz will cry.

204. In the fourteenth paragraph (lines 53–56), why was the lesson different from other lessons for Frantz?

(A) It was an easier lesson than the others.
(B) He concentrated on it more than the others.
(C) He was less concerned about doing well.
(D) It was a lesson that they had done before.

205. What was the author's intention for including the sentence "At the same moment, the bugles of the Prussians returning from drill blared under our windows" (lines 68–69)?

(A) To show that the Prussians were orderly

(B) To suggest that the Prussians marched only in the morning

(C) To show how much people were interested in the Prussians

(D) To suggest how intrusive the Prussians were

206. You can tell that Monsieur Hamel's attitude toward the Prussians was one of

(A) respect.

(B) dislike.

(C) fear.

(D) indifference.

207. When Frantz says that Monsieur Hamel "rose, pale as death" (line 70), he is suggesting that

(A) Monsieur Hamel was dying of a disease.

(B) Monsieur Hamel was embarrassed to be losing his job.

(C) Monsieur Hamel was anemic.

(D) it was like a death for Monsieur Hamel to lose his job.

208. In the twentieth paragraph (line 72), it can reasonably be inferred that Monsieur Hamlin could not finish his sentence because he

(A) forgot what he needed to say.

(B) didn't know what to say.

(C) was losing his voice.

(D) was overcome by emotion.

Paired Passages: Social Sciences

Passage 1: The Journeys of Marco Polo

Marco Polo (1254–1324) was born in the Republic of Venice (known today as Venice, Italy). He is considered one of the greatest explorers in history, traveling to China and learning much about its customs. He is also known to have brought the first spaghetti noodles from China to Venice.

Marco Polo's father, Niccolo, and his uncle, Maffeo, were merchants who traveled and were away from home much of the time; they returned from a trip to China in 1269. There they had met the ruler Kublai Khan, grandson of the Mongol warlord Genghis Khan.

Kublai had expressed interest in learning more about Christianity. He asked   5 Niccolo and Maffeo to return to China with 100 missionaries, so that his people could learn about the religion. Marco wanted to go with them, so in 1271, seventeen-year-old Marco set off with his father and uncle on the long overland route that had become known as the Silk Road: 4,000 miles of very inhospitable terrain with some of the harshest conditions on Earth, vast deserts, and steep 10 mountains. Only two missionaries had agreed to come, but after only a few days, they turned back to Italy. Marco and his party finally arrived after four long years at Xanadu, the summer palace of Kublai Khan, in Inner Mongolia.

The Europeans were awed by what they saw: walls were covered with silver and gold, and there was a great hall where 6,000 people could dine. The emperor had 15 10,000 pure white horses.

After 17 years, Marco wanted to return to Venice. Kublai was getting old; it was feared that if he died, the fortune that the Polo family had amassed over the years would be confiscated. After much badgering, the emperor relented; he would let them depart if they would escort a Mongol princess to Persia to marry a young 20 prince there. In 1292, they left Hangchow to return by sea. The trip lasted three years, and many of the travelers perished in storms or from scurvy. The princess and the Polos did survive, however, and they landed at the port of Hormuz in Persia in 1295.

After returning to Venice, Marco was captured in 1298 while he was com- 25 manding a galley in a war against the rival Republic of Genoa, and he was thrown into a Genoese prison. While in prison, he met the writer Rusticello of Pisa. Marco dictated his adventures to him. When they were released in 1299, Rusticello went on to publish *Description of the World*. Nobody believed the book; they couldn't conceive that such a world as China existed. In Venice, it was called *Il Milione* 30 ("The Million"); the public thought it was made up of a million lies. Marco got the nickname Marco Milione.

A hundred years after his death, handwritten manuscript editions of the book continued to be produced. It was realized that *The Travels of Marco Polo*, as it came to be called, was the most complete rendering of life in Asia that was available in 35 medieval Europe.

A few historians have questioned whether Marco Polo really did go to China, suggesting that he may have only talked with other travelers. There is no mention in the book of the Great Wall of China, for instance, or the custom of binding the feet of women that was prevalent at the time. Nevertheless, *The Travels of Marco* 40 *Polo* has had a profound influence on how Europeans understand a culture so different from their own. In addition, Chinese historians value the book for its detailed insights into thirteenth-century life in China. Marco summed it up for himself, speaking on his deathbed to a priest in 1324, "I have not told half of what I saw."

45

Passage 2: Uncovering a Viking Legacy

If you asked someone who the first European to discover America was, you would probably receive the standard response: Christopher Columbus. However, as time goes on, more and more evidence is uncovered that points to a European presence in North America long before Columbus sailed the ocean blue in 1492.

One of the explorers now credited with visiting North America almost 500 years before Columbus is Leif Ericson. Ericson, who was born about 960 CE, was the son of Eric the Red. The Vikings were known to be a seafaring people. Their raids on the settlements of other countries are legendary. They were also known to be explorers. Ericson's father, Eric the Red, discovered Greenland and   5 led the settlement of that country.

When Ericson was in his twenties, he began learning to travel the deep seas by traveling from Greenland to Norway. There he stayed at King Olav's court and was converted to Christianity. On his return to Greenland he brought a priest with him to spread the Good News.   10

Sometime after he returned from Norway, he decided to sail again. As a young man, Ericson had spoken to another Viking sailor, Bjarni Herjolfsson, who told of a land he had seen west of Greenland: a land that did not have glaciers and was covered with green trees. In hopes of finding that land, Ericson bought Bjarni's boat and raised a crew. He sailed west from Greenland for 600 miles before finally   15 finding an island. They were disappointed in the discovery, however, because it was barren and mostly rock. This is believed to have been what is now known as Baffin Island.

Sailing southward, they reached what is today believed to have been the eastern coast of Canada. Continuing south from there, they finally reached a large island   20 with the mainland behind it. Here, they were rewarded for their travels. They found huge salmon, grassy pastures, and tall forests. They installed temporary shelters and built a large house to winter in.

Ericson named this island Vinland, which is translated either Wineland or Pastureland. Today, we know that island was Newfoundland. Surprisingly, the   25 Vikings did not make a permanent settlement there. The explorers returned to Greenland after the winter was over, and only a few settlers, including Ericson's sister, stayed. Those settlers were later killed by Native Americans. Because of this, the discovery of this new land was not widely known about in Europe.

Although there were Viking legends about Ericson's discovery, it wasn't until   30 1960 that the remnants of Ericson's winter settlement were discovered by archaeologists. That find has become an important historical site known as L'Anse aux Meadows. As a result, the story of Leif Ericson and his travels is finally being told.

Passage 1 Questions

209. In the second paragraph (lines 5–13), it can reasonably be inferred that the two missionaries turned back because they

(A) decided the trip would be too long and hazardous.
(B) were called back by their superiors.
(C) became ill from the strange food.
(D) decided to take a trip elsewhere.

210. The Venetians thought that Marco Polo's book was

    (A) beautifully written.

    (B) a sham.

    (C) too long.

    (D) hard to read.

211. What is the most likely reason that the Mongol princess needed to be escorted to Persia?

    (A) She did not like traveling by herself.

    (B) The trip was too dangerous for a young woman to take on her own.

    (C) She was hesitant to leave her homeland.

    (D) Kublai Khan wanted to make sure she did not run away while traveling.

212. Based on the information in the last paragraph, why do some historians wonder if Marco Polo actually traveled to China?

    (A) He did not bring many things back with him from his travels.

    (B) He was known to make up stories.

    (C) He did not write about the Great Wall of China.

    (D) He was extremely rich.

213. Probably the best proof that Marco Polo did travel to China was

    (A) what he said to the priest.

    (B) the fact that he knew so much about Kublai Khan.

    (C) the fact that he knew how to speak many languages.

    (D) what he told his fellow prisoner.

Passage 2 Questions

214. The author refers to Ericson's Viking heritage as a way to imply

    (A) that Leif was a very violent man.

    (B) that a Viking heritage is something to be proud of.

    (C) that Ericson got his love for exploring naturally.

    (D) that the Vikings were one of the more advanced civilizations at that time.

215. From the passage, it can reasonably be inferred that Ericson was exploring in hopes of finding

    (A) gold and other treasures.

    (B) people to convert to Christianity.

    (C) a new route to India.

    (D) land rich in resources.

216. Based on the information in the passage about Leif Ericson, he was most likely

(A) a man ahead of his time.
(B) someone who liked adventure.
(C) dedicated to the growth of Greenland's settlements.
(D) a cruel and harsh leader.

217. Based on the passage, it could be inferred that the 1960 discovery by archaeologists was important because it

(A) proved that the Viking legends about Ericson were based on truth.
(B) brought much needed tourism to Newfoundland.
(C) allowed historians to have a better understanding of the Viking culture.
(D) made Leif Ericson more famous than Christopher Columbus.

218. The second paragraph of the passage implies that the Vikings were

(A) cruel and ruthless.
(B) willing to leave their homeland.
(C) a people who settled many different lands.
(D) a people who had a long and diverse history.

Paired Passages Questions

219. In which of the following ways does Passage 1 differ from Passage 2?

(A) It follows a chronological timeline.
(B) It quotes the explorer.
(C) It has a more argumentative tone.
(D) It references archaeologists' data.

220. The main point of both passages is to

(A) show that over time our understanding of history changes.
(B) relate the achievements of great explorers.
(C) reveal that Christianity was spread through the efforts of explorers.
(D) illustrate that explorers can change our perception of the world.

221. In which way would the author of Passage 2 most likely respond to this statement from Passage 1: "A few historians have questioned whether Marco Polo really did go to China."

(A) What historians know is continually being challenged by new discoveries.
(B) It is important for historians to come to a consensus in order to educate the populace properly.
(C) Historians should not challenge the stories that have been passed down for generations.
(D) Solid proof should be found one way or the other before the stories of Marco Polo continue to be taught in schools.

222. Which comparison of the passages is the most accurate?

(A) Passage 1 indicates that sea travel was dangerous, while Passage 2 indicates that it was relatively safe.

(B) Passage 1 implies that only proven historical facts should be trusted, while Passage 2 implies that legends should be given more credence.

(C) Both passages imply that stories often contain more truth than they are credited with.

(D) Both passages indicate that spreading Christianity was the driving force behind exploration.

Humanities

"The Snow-Walkers" by John Burroughs

This excerpt is adapted from an essay in *In the Catskills* by John Burroughs (1837–1921), an American naturalist and essayist. Burroughs built a cabin in the woods in the Catskill Mountains area of New York State. He did most of his writing at the cabin, called Slabsides, which is now a National Historic Landmark.

He who marvels at the beauty of the world in summer will find equal cause for wonder and admiration in winter. It is true the pomp and the pageantry are swept away, but the essential elements remain,—the day and the night, the mountain and the valley, the elemental play and succession and the perpetual presence of the infinite sky. In winter the stars seem to have rekindled their fires, the moon   5
achieves a fuller triumph, and the heavens wear a look of a more exalted simplicity. Summer is more wooing and seductive, more versatile and human, appeals to the affections and the sentiments, and fosters inquiry and the art impulse. Winter is of a more heroic cast, and addresses the intellect. The severe studies and disciplines come easier in winter. One imposes larger tasks upon himself, and is less tolerant   10
of his own weaknesses.

The tendinous part of the mind, so to speak, is more developed in winter; the fleshy, in summer. I should say winter had given the bone and sinew to Literature, summer the tissues and blood.

The simplicity of winter has a deep moral. The return of nature, after such a   15
career of splendor and prodigality, to habits so simple and austere, is not lost either upon the head or the heart. It is the philosopher coming back from the banquet and the wine to a cup of water and a crust of bread.

And then this beautiful masquerade of the elements,—the novel disguises our nearest friends put on! Here is another rain and another dew, water that will not   20
flow, nor spill, nor receive the taint of an unclean vessel. And if we see truly, the same old beneficence and willingness to serve lurk beneath all.

Look up at the miracle of the falling snow,—the air a dizzy maze of whirling, eddying flakes, noiselessly transforming the world, the exquisite crystals dropping in ditch and gutter, and disguising in the same suit of spotless livery all objects   25 upon which they fall. How novel and fine the first drifts! The old, dilapidated fence is suddenly set off with the most fantastic ruffles, scalloped and fluted after an unheard-of fashion! Looking down a long line of decrepit stone wall, in the trimming of which the wind had fairly run riot, I saw, as for the first time, what a severe yet master artist old Winter is. Ah, a severe artist! How stern the woods look, 30 dark and cold and as rigid against the horizon as iron!

All life and action upon the snow have an added emphasis and significance. Every expression is underscored. Summer has few finer pictures than this winter one of the farmer foddering his cattle from a stack upon the clean snow,—the movement, the sharply defined figures, the great green flakes of hay, the long file of 35 patient cows, the advance just arriving and pressing eagerly for the choicest morsels, and the bounty and providence it suggests. Or the chopper in the woods,—the prostrate tree, the white new chips scattered about, his easy triumph over the cold, his coat hanging to a limb, and the clear, sharp ring of his axe. The woods are rigid and tense, keyed up by the frost, and resound like a stringed instrument. Or the 40 road-breakers, sallying forth with oxen and sleds in the still, white world, the day after the storm, to restore the lost track and demolish the beleaguering drifts.

All sounds are sharper in winter; the air transmits better. At night I hear more distinctly the steady roar of the North Mountain. In summer it is a sort of complacent purr, as the breezes stroke down its sides; but in winter always the same 45 low, sullen growl.

A severe artist! No longer the canvas and the pigments, but the marble and the chisel. When the nights are calm and the moon full, I go out to gaze upon the wonderful purity of the moonlight and the snow. The air is full of latent fire, and the cold warms me—after a different fashion from that of the kitchen stove. The 50 world lies about me in a "trance of snow." The clouds are pearly and iridescent, and seem the farthest possible remove from the condition of a storm,—the ghosts of clouds, the indwelling beauty freed from all dross. I see the hills, bulging with great drifts, lift themselves up cold and white against the sky, the black lines of fences here and there obliterated by the depth of the snow. Presently a fox barks away up 55 next the mountain, and I imagine I can almost see him sitting there, in his furs, upon the illuminated surface, and looking down in my direction. As I listen, one answers him from behind the woods in the valley. What a wild winter sound, wild and weird, up among the ghostly hills! Since the wolf has ceased to howl upon these mountains, and the panther to scream, there is nothing to be compared with 60 it. So wild! I get up in the middle of the night to hear it. It is refreshing to the ear, and one delights to know that such wild creatures are among us. At this season Nature makes the most of every throb of life that can withstand her severity. How heartily she indorses this fox! In what bold relief stand out the lives of all walkers of the snow! The snow is a great tell-tale, and blabs as effectually as it obliterates. 65 I go into the woods, and know all that has happened. I cross the fields, and if only a mouse has visited his neighbor, the fact is chronicled.

223. According to the author, what effect does winter have on the moon?

    (A)　It seems more silver.

    (B)　Its terrain looks smoother.

    (C)　It seems bigger.

    (D)　Its light is dimmed.

224. It can reasonably be inferred that "the tendinous part of the mind" (line 12) refers to the

    (A)　imagination that creates beauty.

    (B)　ligaments that hold things together.

    (C)　passion that creates drama.

    (D)　sadness that causes intensity.

225. Summer is described by the author in all of the following ways EXCEPT

    (A)　intelligent.

    (B)　seductive.

    (C)　versatile.

    (D)　human.

226. According to the author, which of the following activities is most likely done during the winter?

    (A)　Reading philosophy

    (B)　Writing a play

    (C)　Falling in love

    (D)　Holding a seminar

227. The main point of the third paragraph (lines 15–18) is that winter

    (A)　is a victim of summer.

    (B)　gives less joy than summer.

    (C)　cleanses the individual.

    (D)　is harder to live through.

228. Which words best describe the author?

    (A)　Overwrought and tense

    (B)　Pragmatic and intellectual

    (C)　Romantic and deep-seeing

    (D)　Cynical and despairing

229. The main point of the fifth paragraph (lines 23–31) is that the snow

    (A)　makes the stone fence look like iron.

    (B)　transforms ordinary objects into something wonderful.

    (C)　is difficult to describe.

    (D)　makes everything look cold.

230. When the author speaks of the chopper's "easy triumph over the cold" (line 38), he means that

(A) the chopper wears a heavy sweater.

(B) the work of cutting trees keeps the chopper warm.

(C) the trees protect the chopper from the wind.

(D) it is not very cold.

231. From the information in the seventh paragraph (lines 43–46), it can reasonably be inferred that cold air

(A) helps sound travel.

(B) keeps noises quieter.

(C) makes higher sounds.

(D) helps create strong feelings.

232. When the author says that "the air is full of latent fire" (line 49), he means that the air

(A) makes it easier to build a fire.

(B) is extremely dry.

(C) burns the lungs when a person breathes.

(D) contains a hidden warmth.

233. The author views the sound of the fox as

(A) annoying at night.

(B) frightening to hear in the winter.

(C) chilling.

(D) inspiring.

234. The author likens winter to a(n)

(A) fox.

(B) artist.

(C) poet.

(D) farmer.

235. The author describes winter in all of the following ways EXCEPT

(A) austere.

(B) severe.

(C) sentimental.

(D) essential.

236. When the author says, "if only a mouse has visited his neighbor, the fact is chronicled" (lines 66–67), he means that

(A) no one would ever know.
(B) there is food in the snow.
(C) it would make noises.
(D) its footprints would be recorded in the snow.

Natural Sciences

Eaters of Light

Black holes are a part of the universe that have intrigued scientists for many years. This passage addresses what scientists have slowly uncovered about these phenomena.

What is a black hole? A black hole is an area in space where the force of gravity is so strong that light cannot get out. It is basically a dead star. The star itself has disappeared; what is left is the gravity. An enormous amount of matter is intensely compressed and squeezed into a small space.

The phrase "black hole" was first used by physicist John Archibald Wheeler in 1967. Until that time, black holes were just a theory; their existence had not been proven, nor had a black hole been observed, since there is nothing to "see." The existence of black holes was foreshadowed by Albert Einstein. In his *General Theory of Relativity*, published in 1915, he proposed that gravity is not a force, as had previously been accepted since the time of Sir Isaac Newton in the seventeenth century, but a consequence of distortion in space and time—what he called "space-time."

Einstein's theory led scientists to ponder what the effect of matter enormously compressed would have on gravity and energy. At the time, it was presumed that this was impossible. In the 1960s, theoretical scientists confirmed that black holes were a prediction of general relativity.

Since that time, by studying how stars and interstellar gases orbit black holes and by using radio telescopes, scientists have been able to measure black holes. By measuring the speed of the material orbiting the black hole and the size of the orbit, scientists can determine the mass of the black hole using the laws of gravity. What they have found is that the size of black holes ranges from tiny to supermassive.

As a dead star collapses on itself, the mass becomes so tremendous that it bends space and time around itself. Nothing can get out. This infinitely dense region is called a singularity. It cannot be measured, since it is equal to infinity. An event horizon is a spherical boundary outside the black hole where the gravitational attraction nearly equals the speed of light.

It is now believed that every large galaxy has at least one supermassive black hole at its center. Our own galaxy, the Milky Way, has one. Called Sagittarius A* (read as "Sagittarius A Star" and abbreviated *Sgr A**), it is 27,000 light years from Earth and has a mass equal to four million suns, with a diameter (event horizon) of 24 million miles. In comparison, Earth is 93 million miles from the sun.

Scientists have been able to analyze event horizons in space using the Chandra X-ray Observatory. Launched by NASA in 1999 by the Space Shuttle *Columbia* (under the command of the first woman to command a mission, Eileen Collins), Chandra has a resolution so acute that it is equivalent to being able to read a stop sign from a distance of 12 miles. X-rays have a shorter wavelength than visible 35 light, so X-rays transmitted from space cannot be measured on Earth—they are absorbed by the atmosphere. The Chandra X-ray Observatory orbits the Earth at a distance of 86,500 miles; it can observe X-rays from particles heated to 180 million degrees Fahrenheit right up to the last second before they are sucked into a black hole. 40

NASA's Nuclear Spectroscopic Telescope Array (NuSTAR), launched in 2012, measures high-energy X-ray light. It has recorded flares on the surface of Sgr A* as the black hole gobbles up matter. NuSTAR will conduct a census of black holes and probe the origin of cosmic rays.

Some people believe that black holes are "wormholes" that lead to another 45 dimension and another universe. There is no way to prove such a theory, because nothing would be able to enter a black hole and survive. One physicist, Nikodem Popławski, has put forth a theory that the matter contained in such infinite density at the center of a black hole is actually spewn out the other side, which he calls a white hole, where it forms the basic building blocks for another universe in a 50 reality different from ours. It is possible that there may be an infinite number of universes in addition to the one we call home.

Dr. Wheeler summed up existing knowledge about black holes in his 1999 autobiography, *Geons, Black Holes, and Quantum Foam: A Life in Physics*: A black hole "teaches us that space can be crumpled up like paper into an infinitesimal dot, 55 that time can be extinguished like a blown-out flame, and that the laws of physics that we regard as 'sacred,' as immutable, are anything but."

237. According to the passage, a black hole has all of the following characteristics EXCEPT

(A) a distortion in space and time.
(B) a tremendous force of gravity.
(C) intensely compressed matter.
(D) the inability of light to get out.

238. Which of the following scientists is credited with first theorizing the existence of black holes?

(A) John Wheeler
(B) Isaac Newton
(C) Nikodem Popławski
(D) Albert Einstein

239. Which of the following statements best describes the function of NuSTAR?

    (A) It predicts the existence of compressed matter.

    (B) It calculates the event horizon.

    (C) It measures high-energy X-rays.

    (D) It maps the event horizon of Sgr A*.

240. According to the passage, scientists measure black holes by

    (A) bending space and time around them.

    (B) studying the movement of stars around them.

    (C) observing X-ray emissions from flares.

    (D) defining the singularity of a black hole.

241. As described in the passage, Chandra allows scientists to

    (A) read a stop sign from a distance of 12 miles.

    (B) confirm Einstein's theory of relativity.

    (C) analyze data that cannot be obtained on Earth.

    (D) prove that wormholes exist.

242. It can reasonably be inferred that the author of the passage believes that

    (A) black holes cannot be seen, but they can be measured.

    (B) Einstein was a genius, truly a man ahead of his time.

    (C) the nature of the universe may never be fully understood.

    (D) the size of supermassive black holes boggles the mind.

243. According to the passage, when a dead star collapses, it

    (A) becomes unbelievably dense in mass.

    (B) emits measurable high-energy X-rays.

    (C) becomes a supermassive black hole.

    (D) reaches a temperature of 180 million degrees Fahrenheit.

244. It can reasonably be inferred from the sixth paragraph (lines 26–30) that

    (A) Sgr A* has a diameter of about one-fourth the distance between Earth and the sun.

    (B) the Milky Way has a supermassive black hole at its center.

    (C) Sgr A* has a mass equivalent to 27,000 suns.

    (D) the event horizon of a black hole is the same as its diameter.

245. According to the passage, Isaac Newton

    (A) first coined the phrase "black hole."

    (B) defined gravity as a force.

    (C) discovered the Milky Way.

    (D) had a satellite named after him.

246. According to the passage, the difference between a wormhole and a black hole is that

(A) black holes cannot be seen.

(B) black holes eject matter out the other side.

(C) wormholes could lead to a parallel universe.

(D) wormholes are just a fantasy.

247. In the passage, the author refers to physicist John Archibald Wheeler as being best known for

(A) *Geons, Black Holes, and Quantum Foam: A Life in Physics.*

(B) confirming that Einstein predicted black holes.

(C) the invention of the radio telescope.

(D) first using the term "black hole" in scientific circles.

248. The main point of the ninth paragraph (lines 45–52) is that

(A) there is at least one other universe in existence besides ours.

(B) so-called wormholes have yet to be discovered.

(C) black holes contain the building blocks for new universes.

(D) any theory about where a black hole might lead cannot be proved.

249. Based on the information in the passage, it can reasonably be inferred that if you were to approach a black hole in a spaceship and you traveled inside the event horizon,

(A) you would be able to see if wormholes actually exist.

(B) you could measure the X-rays emitted from the singularity.

(C) the gravitational pull would overwhelm you.

(D) space-time would no longer exist.

250. When Dr. Wheeler says that "the laws of physics that we regard as 'sacred,' as immutable, are anything but" (lines 56–57), he means that the laws of physics are

(A) ignorant.

(B) permanent.

(C) variable.

(D) itinerant.

PART 2

English

CHAPTER 5

Set 1 English Questions

In the passages that follow, certain words and phrases are underlined and numbered. Each number refers to a question that offers alternatives for the underlined word or phrase. In most cases, you are to choose the answer that best expresses the idea, makes the statement appropriate for standard written English, or is worded most consistently with the style and tone of the passage as a whole. If you think that the original version is best, choose "NO CHANGE."

There are also questions about a section of the passage or about the passage as a whole. These questions do not refer to an underlined portion of the passage, but are identified by numbers in boxes.

Alice Paul: Suffragette

Suffragette Alice Paul was born in New Jersey in 1885. She went on to found the National Women's Party and dedicate her entire life to the cause
                                    251
that men and women should be equal in society. Although raised as a
                                                  252
Quaker, she believed, like all Quakers, in gender equality. Even as a child,

she attended meetings of the American Suffrage Association. Paul had an

exceptionally keen mind. She earned a B.A. from Swarthmore College in

1905, an M.A. and a Ph.D. from the University of Pennsylvania in 1907 and

1912 and three law degrees from American University—a bachelor, masters,
253
and doctor of law in the 1920s.

Paul having traveled to England in 1907. It was there that she met the
          254
militant suffragette Emmeline Pankhurst, who believed that prayers and
                                                       255

petitions were not enough and that action was needed. As they were arrested
<u> </u>
256
and imprisoned several times, but their actions resulted in newspaper stories that

brought their struggle out into the open. <u>In prison</u>, Paul would take comfort
257
from Thomas Jefferson's words, "Resistance to tyranny is obedience to God."

[1] Paul returned to the U.S. in 1910. [2] It was in 1916 that she founded

the National Women's Party. [3] She and others became famous for what the

press called "Silent Sentinels." 258 [4] They were arrested many times, <u>while</u>
259
the tactic brought them publicity, and ceding to the public outcry, President

Woodrow Wilson <u>reversing</u> his position against equal rights. [5] The women
260
would stand outside the White House day after day bearing banners <u>demanded</u>
261
equal rights. [6] Congress passed the Nineteenth Amendment: "The right of

citizens of the United States to vote shall <u>not be, denied or abridged, by</u> the
262
United States or by any State on account of sex." [7] The <u>amendment was ratified</u>
263
and became law on August 26, 1920. 264

In the 1920s, Paul <u>continues</u> to champion women's rights, proposing an
265
Equal Rights Amendment that guaranteed absolute equality. She founded the

Women's World Party in 1938, based in Geneva, Switzerland, and traveled all

over the world. She worked to ensure that gender equality was included in the

United Nations Charter.

The Equal Rights Amendment (ERA) was finally passed by Congress in 1972.

Paul died on July 9, 1977.

The <u>ERA yet has</u> not been ratified, needing approval by three more states
266
before it can become the Twenty-eighth Amendment.

251. (A) NO CHANGE
    (B) Party, and
    (C) Party; and
    (D) Party and,

252. (A) NO CHANGE
    (B) While
    (C) When
    (D) OMIT the underlined portion.

253. (A) NO CHANGE
    (B) 1912; and
    (C) 1912: and
    (D) 1912, and

254. (A) NO CHANGE
    (B) had traveled
    (C) was traveling
    (D) OMIT the underlined portion.

255. (A) NO CHANGE
    (B) believing
    (C) having believed
    (D) was believing

256. (A) NO CHANGE
    (B) After
    (C) When
    (D) OMIT the underlined portion.

257. (A) NO CHANGE
    (B) When in prison
    (C) After being in prison
    (D) While in prison

258. The writer is considering revising the last part of the preceding sentence ("for what the press called 'Silent Sentinels' ") to read as "for their demonstrations." If the writer did this, the essay would primarily lose

    (A) Paul's purpose for the demonstrations.
    (B) the idea that Paul was not demonstrating alone.
    (C) Paul's description of the demonstrations.
    (D) the name given to the demonstrations by the media.

259. (A) NO CHANGE
     (B) but
     (C) since
     (D) OMIT the underlined portion.

260. (A) NO CHANGE
     (B) reversed
     (C) was reversing
     (D) has reversed

261. (A) NO CHANGE
     (B) demanding
     (C) are demanding
     (D) was demanding

262. (A) NO CHANGE
     (B) not be denied or abridged, by
     (C) not be, denied or abridged by state on
     (D) not be denied or abridged by

263. (A) NO CHANGE
     (B) amendment ratified
     (C) amendment is being ratified
     (D) amendment is ratified

264. For the sake of the logic and coherence of the paragraph, Sentence 5 should be
     (A) placed where it is now.
     (B) placed after Sentence 3.
     (C) placed after Sentence 6.
     (D) OMITTED from the paragraph.

265. (A) NO CHANGE
     (B) is continuing
     (C) continued
     (D) will continue

266. (A) NO CHANGE
     (B) ERA but has
     (C) ERA still has
     (D) ERA that has

Life at the South Pole

The Amundsen-Scott South Pole Station is situated at the Geographic South Pole on the Antarctic Continent. It is <u>absolutely the most southern place</u> on the
<u>267</u>
Earth. The facility is named after the first two men to reach the South Pole just months apart: <u>they were</u> the Norwegian explorer Roald Amundsen, who arrived
<u>268</u>
on December 14, 1911, and Robert F. Scott of Great Britain, who reached the South Pole on January 17, 1912. Tragically, Scott and his party died <u>from exposure</u> on their return journey. It wasn't until 1956 that the United
<u>269</u>
States opened a research facility at the South Pole. The current station, the third on the site, was completed in 2008 and is elevated on stilts so it cannot be buried by drifting snow.

Located at an elevation of <u>just exactly 9,306 feet</u>, the station sits above
<u>270</u>
a sheet of ice 9,000 feet thick. Conditions are <u>difficult</u>; during the six months
<u>271</u>
from April to September, which is winter in the South Pole, the sun never shines and the temperature falls to 100 degrees below zero. <u>Consequently</u>, during this
<u>272</u>
period 50 or so scientists remain at the station, but during the summer, the population <u>gets</u> to over 150.
<u>273</u>
In spite of being located in such a remote place, the Amundsen-Scott South Pole Station is alive with numerous scientific studies. 274 This is because the station is a prime location for research for a number of scientific disciplines, <u>all of which are represented with experiments.</u>
<u>275</u>
The Martin A. Pomerantz Observatory, known as MAPO, was named after the astronomer who first realized the value of Antarctica for telescopes because of its cleaner, thinner <u>and has no light pollution atmosphere</u>, spends the long
<u>276</u>

winter night searching the skies. The observatory is a two-story elevated structure and is home to equipment that operates and supports four projects: the Antarctic Muon and Neutrino Detector Array (AMANDA), the South Pole Infrared Explorer (SPIREX), the Cosmic Background Radiation Anisotropy (COBRA) experiment, and the Advanced Telescope Project (ATP). 277

Nearby, the radio telescope probes the universe for dark matter. Not far from the observatory is the world's largest neutrino detector. Called IceCube it
278
is buried one and a half miles below the surface identifying neutrinos, charged, subatomic particles that arise from exploding stars, black holes, and, also,
279
neutron stars and travel at the speed of light. The electromagnetic radiation they emit when they hit the ice is analyzed by computers on the surface. However,
280
scientists are hoping to discover the origin of high-energy cosmic rays.

Scientists from all over the world takes advantage of the unique conditions
281
the continent provides to conduct their research. Altogether, 30 countries maintain permanent or seasonal facilities on the Antarctic Ice Shelf. 282

267. (A) NO CHANGE
 (B) so very far south
 (C) just the most southern point
 (D) the southernmost point

268. (A) NO CHANGE
 (B) they had been
 (C) they were being
 (D) OMIT the underlined portion.

269. (A) NO CHANGE
 (B) from the very cold weather they were having
 (C) from not having enough warm clothes
 (D) from the way they had to travel over ice

270. (A) NO CHANGE
    (B) exactly around 9,306 feet
    (C) about 9,306 feet
    (D) 9,306 feet

271. Given that all of the choices are true, which one best emphasizes the extent of the difficulty of the weather in the South Pole?
    (A) NO CHANGE
    (B) extremely severe and life-threatening
    (C) hard to deal with
    (D) freezing cold most of the time

272. Which of the following alternatives to the underlined portion would NOT be acceptable?
    (A) As a result
    (B) Accordingly
    (C) Because of this
    (D) In spite of this

273. (A) NO CHANGE
    (B) swells
    (C) grows
    (D) increases

274. If the writer were to delete the words *remote* and *numerous* from the preceding sentence, the sentence would primarily lose
    (A) a feeling that the station is open to everyone.
    (B) a suggestion of the nature of the scientific research that goes on in the station.
    (C) a contrast between the location and the number of scientists working there.
    (D) a sense of where the station is in Antarctica.

275. Given that all of the choices are true, which one best supports the sentence's claim about the Amundsen-Scott South Pole Station's being a prime location for a number of scientific disciplines?
    (A) NO CHANGE
    (B) all of which come from many countries.
    (C) such as geology, biology, astrophysics, and oceanography.
    (D) but no one owns the continent of Antarctica.

276. (A) NO CHANGE
    (B) and a no light pollution atmosphere,
    (C) atmosphere with no pollution,
    (D) atmosphere that has no light pollution at all,

277. At this point, the writer is considering adding the following true statement:

> Pomerantz was one of the pioneers in balloon-borne cosmic ray research in the 1940s and 1950s.

Should the writer make this addition here?
    (A) Yes, because it tells more about who Pomerantz was.
    (B) Yes, because it fits in with the overall point of the essay.
    (C) No, because it doesn't tell enough about why the observatory was named for Pomerantz.
    (D) No, because the information would be off the main topic of what the observatory does.

278. (A) NO CHANGE
    (B) IceCube, it
    (C) IceCube. It
    (D) IceCube; it

279. (A) NO CHANGE
    (B) and
    (C) and as well,
    (D) and too

280. (A) NO CHANGE
    (B) Because
    (C) As a result,
    (D) OMIT the underlined portion.

281. (A) NO CHANGE
    (B) take
    (C) has taken
    (D) OMIT the underlined portion.

282. If the writer were to delete the phrase "permanent or seasonal" from the preceding sentence, the sentence would primarily lose

(A) the feeling that many scientists prefer not to use the facilities.

(B) the notion that most facilities are permanent.

(C) the suggestion that most scientists work during the winter months.

(D) the idea that not all of the scientific facilities operate full-time.

El Yunque

El Yunque National Forest is the only tropical rain forest in the United States. This marvelous attraction, located near the eastern end of Puerto Rico, has been a part of the U.S. National Forest Service <u>from as long ago as</u> 1903. Part of the
283
Sierra de Luquillo Mountain <u>Range, El Yunque</u> covers over 28,000 acres.
284
The mountain itself has an elevation of 3,543 feet and offers <u>some of the better</u> views of the surrounding areas.
285

The name "El Yunque" comes from a Taino word, *Yuque*, meaning "white lands." The Taino, who were native to the island, named the rain forest "Yuque" because there were always <u>big flowing</u> white clouds surrounding the mountain
286
at the center of the forest. These people believed that a god <u>in the mountain</u> lived
287
and that he would protect them.

Climbing up the <u>mountains slope,</u> visitors can see Yokahu Tower. At an
288
elevation of 1,900 feet and 70 feet high, the tower offers a magnificent panoramic view of the Atlantic Ocean and San Juan, the capital of Puerto Rico. El Yunque's peak, <u>which was earlier noted</u>, is almost always <u>within</u> clouds and mist, averages
289   290
over 240 inches of rain a year. <u>Incredibly,</u> there are 175 tree species in El Yunque,
291
23 of which are only found there, and 150 species of ferns. Exotic vegetation like the Palo Colorado Palm and the Giant Tree Fern thrive, and dozens of brightly colored bromeliad varieties abound. [292]

Visitors can explore the many hiking trails in the park, <u>of which there are many.</u> El Yunque Rock, a massive outcropping rising above
—— 293

the forest, is a popular destination. Other attractions include the many waterfalls and rocky pools. La Coca Falls has a spectacular drop of 185 feet. The water temperature remains at about 60 degrees all year round, and visitors often enjoy a dip in the crystal waters at its base before continuing their hike.

[1] So many creatures abound in El Yunque. [2] <u>Its</u> home to the Puerto Rican
                                                —— 294
Parrot, *Amazona vittata,* which is bright green, with white-ringed eyes and <u>around the beak</u> a brilliant red. [3] Puerto Rico once was filled with the bird.
—— 295
[4] Conservation efforts began in 1968, and today there are more than 40 in El Yunque and over 100 in captivity. [5] But civilization encroached and, by the 1960s, there were only two dozen left. [6] El Yunque also has 13 species of coquí, the tiny tree frog found all over the island, and loved for its unique call, which sounds like its name. [7] The call <u>rings out</u> from dusk until dawn each night.
                                                            —— 296
It is a sound that all Puerto Ricans love. ⌐297⌐

A visit to El Yunque will give one a sense of the way that the early Taino people must have viewed this special place, which they thought of as magical; it is certainly a must-see for every visitor. ⌐298⌐

283. (A) NO CHANGE
    (B) as far back as
    (C) since
    (D) OMIT the underlined portion.

284. (A) NO CHANGE
    (B) Range El Yunque
    (C) Range. El Yunque
    (D) Range; El Yunque

285. (A) NO CHANGE
     (B) long vistas
     (C) astonishing
     (D) OMIT the underlined portion.

286. (A) NO CHANGE
     (B) many
     (C) large
     (D) billowy

287. The best placement for the underlined portion would be
     (A) where it is now.
     (B) before the word *god.*
     (C) before the word *and.*
     (D) before the word *that.*

288. (A) NO CHANGE
     (B) mountains slope
     (C) mountains' slope,
     (D) mountain's slope,

289. (A) NO CHANGE
     (B) which the writer had earlier stated about the mountain
     (C) which the reader learned in the preceding paragraph
     (D) which was mentioned earlier on in the essay

290. (A) NO CHANGE
     (B) shrouded in
     (C) covered up with
     (D) OMIT the underlined portion.

291. (A) NO CHANGE
     (B) However
     (C) Realistically
     (D) OMIT the underlined portion.

292. If the writer were to delete the word *exotic* from the preceding sentence, the sentence would primarily lose
     (A) a firm understanding of the extent of vegetation in El Yunque.
     (B) the contrast between the forms of vegetation and tree variety.
     (C) the thought that El Yunque has many forms of vegetation.
     (D) the suggestion that these are not everyday forms of vegetation.

293. Given that all of the choices are true, which one provides the most significant new information?

    (A) NO CHANGE
    (B) which are rated at levels from easy to strenuous.
    (C) which are found all over the forest.
    (D) which are enjoyed by many people.

294. (A) NO CHANGE
    (B) It's
    (C) Its'
    (D) OMIT the underlined portion.

295. The best placement for the underlined portion would be

    (A) where it is now.
    (B) after the word *eyes*.
    (C) after the word *brilliant*.
    (D) after the word *red*.

296. (A) NO CHANGE
    (B) continues
    (C) says
    (D) declares

297. For the sake of the logic and coherence of the paragraph, Sentence 5 should be placed

    (A) where it is now.
    (B) after Sentence 1.
    (C) after Sentence 3.
    (D) after Sentence 6.

298. If the writer were to change the pronoun *one* to *you* in the preceding sentence, this closing sentence would

    (A) suggest that the writer is trying to tell the reader what to do.
    (B) make the essay's audience feel uncomfortable.
    (C) create a more appealing and personal tone.
    (D) indicate that the writer is confused.

The Life of Abdul Rahman

The story of the life of Abdul Rahman is a strange and tragic one.

He was born in <u>Timbuktu, a famous city in western Africa</u> in 1769.
299

His father was the king of Futa Jallon, a small kingdom near Timbuktu.

Abdul was heir to the throne and was educated to be a <u>king, he</u> studied
300

geography, mathematics, astronomy, and the history and laws of his country.

<u>He was also a student of Islam, his religion.</u>
301

The first white man Abdul <u>ever seen</u> was John C. Cox, an English surgeon
302

who traveled through their kingdom. Cox became ill with malaria and

recuperated at the court of Abdul's father. Cox stayed for <u>six months time.</u>
303

During that time, Cox <u>learned about the culture.</u> When he felt better and
304

wanted to return to England, the king <u>paying his fare</u> and sent men to escort
305

him safely to the ship.

[1] Seven years later, Abdul <u>was taking</u> prisoner and sold as a slave in
306

Natchez, Mississippi. [2] Abdul, <u>that was called Prince</u>, worked in the fields
307

with other slaves. [3] John Cox happened to visit Mississippi and found Abdul.

[4] Seventeen years passed. [5] He tried to buy his friend's freedom, but was

unsuccessful. 308

Abdul's master would not sell this slave, his <u>more</u> productive one.
309

Finally, in 1829, Abdul and his wife were freed and sent with 160 other

African-Americans <u>to live</u> in Liberia, a country on the west coast of Africa.
310

Liberia was a new country set up in 1822 by the American Colonization Society

to provide a home for freed slaves from America. 311 Abdul's job in his new

country was developing trade and good relations with nearby African nations

<u>through diplomacy.</u>
312

He wrote to his relatives to get money to free his children and grandchildren
<u>   </u>
                                         313
from enslavement in America. Some men were given $7,000 in gold to bring to
<u>   </u>
         313
Abdul. <u>However before</u> they reached Liberia, they were told that Abdul was dead.
         314

Unfortunately for Abdul's children, they decided to return home with the gold.

The African historian Professor Kazembe has said, "The sad story of Abdul

Rahman symbolizes the tragedy of slavery." This tragedy was recently featured in

a made-for-TV movie that depicted the importance of Abdul's life.

299. (A) NO CHANGE
    (B) Timbuktu, a famous city in western Africa,
    (C) Timbuktu; a famous city in western Africa
    (D) Timbuktu a famous city in Western Africa

300. (A) NO CHANGE
    (B) king; he
    (C) king—he
    (D) king. He

301. Which choice would most effectively conclude this paragraph?
    (A) NO CHANGE
    (B) The history of his country was complicated.
    (C) He was a good student and became knowledgeable about many
         things.
    (D) Islam was the predominant religion of his country.

302. (A) NO CHANGE
    (B) ever saw
    (C) ever had seen
    (D) ever had been seen

303. (A) NO CHANGE
    (B) six months' time
    (C) six month's time
    (D) six month times

304. Given that all of the choices are true, which choice provides more information that is relevant and that makes the rest of the essay understandable?

 (A) NO CHANGE
 (B) Cox became good friends with young Abdul.
 (C) Cox met with many different people.
 (D) Cox learned about Islam.

305. (A) NO CHANGE
 (B) paid his fare
 (C) was paying his fare
 (D) has paid his fare

306. (A) NO CHANGE
 (B) was taken
 (C) had been taken
 (D) taken

307. (A) NO CHANGE
 (B) who was called Prince
 (C) whom was called Prince
 (D) which was called Prince

308. Which of the following sequences of sentences makes the paragraph most logical?

 (A) NO CHANGE
 (B) 1, 4, 2, 5, 3
 (C) 2, 1, 3, 4, 5
 (D) 1, 2, 4, 3, 5

309. (A) NO CHANGE
 (B) most
 (C) mostest
 (D) OMIT the underlined portion.

310. (A) NO CHANGE
 (B) to be living
 (C) who live
 (D) to lived

311. If the writer were to delete the phrase "by the American Colonization Society," the passage would lose a detail that
    (A) shows that Liberians were magnanimous about accepting freed slaves.
    (B) lends historical accuracy to the paragraph.
    (C) is critical of the efforts of Americans to colonize Liberia.
    (D) provides an origin for the meaning of the word *Liberia*.

312. The best placement for the underlined portion would be
    (A) where it is now.
    (B) after the word *developing*.
    (C) after the word *country*.
    (D) after the word *relations*.

313. (A) NO CHANGE
    (B) Wanting to get his children and grandchildren free from slavery in America, he wrote to his relatives to get money.
    (C) To get his children and grandchildren freed from slavery in America, he wanted to write to his relatives to get money.
    (D) To get money, he wrote to his relatives to free his children and grandchildren from enslavement in America.

314. (A) NO CHANGE
    (B) However, before
    (C) However—before
    (D) However; before

Tsunamis

Note: The following paragraphs may not be in the most logical order. Each paragraph is numbered; question 330 asks you to choose where Paragraph 2 would most logically be placed.

[1] Tsunamis can occur in any ocean, most are in the Pacific Ocean,
                                  ‾‾‾‾‾‾‾‾‾‾‾
                                      315
where there were many quakes in the sea and on land. The Pacific Ocean
           ‾‾‾‾
            316
strongly affected by volcanoes. A volcano or earthquake may create a tsunami
‾‾‾‾‾‾‾‾‾‾‾‾‾‾‾‾
      317
in the ocean thousands of miles away. The majority of tsunamis occur near

Hawaii, Alaska, Japan, and the West Coast of the United States. The explosion

of the volcano <u>Krakatoa, near Java, in 1883,</u> resulted in a tsunami that killed
                 318

36,000 people many miles from there.

[2] Imagine a wall of ocean water reaching 100 feet high. This wave

crashes onto the shore, crushing buildings and washing thousands of people

out to sea. Scientists <u>call this amazing phenomenon of the ocean</u>
                                   319

a tsunami; <u>Japanese for "storm wave."</u> It destroys towns and kills thousands
           320

of people. Tsunamis are also known as tidal waves, although <u>it has</u> nothing to
                                            321

do with actual tides. 322

[3] What causes this horrifying disaster? The cause can be either an undersea

earthquake, called a seaquake <u>more often,</u> or a volcanic eruption or earthquake
                                323

on land. Oceanographer Patrick Martin says, "A tsunami is created when a quake

causes land <u>shifted</u> underwater." When a tsunami begins, it creates low waves
            324

that speed along at up to 500 miles per <u>hour. However,</u> this doesn't immediately
                                    325

cause huge waves to form out on the ocean. Instead, these small swells of water

rush along and then turn into a huge wave near land. As the ocean becomes

<u>shallowest,</u> the tsunami near the shore builds up, pulling water up with it and
   326

<u>exposes</u> the sea bottom. Then the tsunami strikes the shore with devastating
   327

force.

[4] The Pacific Tsunami Warning Center in Hawaii monitors seaquakes and

<u>sent out</u> warnings of tsunamis. Scientists use seismographs (machines that detect
   328

and measure quakes) to predict where and when a tsunami will strike. This early

warning system cannot prevent tsunamis, although <u>it's been</u> successful in saving
                                        329

lives. One of the newest ways to track tsunamis is with satellites. Scientists use

satellites to track the beginnings and movements of tsunamis all over the

world. 330

315. (A) NO CHANGE
   (B) ocean most
   (C) ocean. Most
   (D) ocean—most

316. (A) NO CHANGE
   (B) have been
   (C) will be
   (D) are

317. (A) NO CHANGE
   (B) will be strongly affected
   (C) strongly affect
   (D) can be strongly affected

318. (A) NO CHANGE
   (B) Krakatoa; near Java in 1883,
   (C) Krakatoa near Java, in 1883,
   (D) Krakatoa, near Java; in 1883.

319. Which of the choices best emphasizes the damage a tsunami can cause?
   (A) NO CHANGE
   (B) call this terror of the ocean
   (C) label this force of nature
   (D) have given it a name—

320. (A) NO CHANGE
   (B) . Japanese for "storm wave."
   (C) : Japanese for "storm wave."
   (D) Japanese for "storm wave."

321. (A) NO CHANGE
   (B) it had
   (C) they had
   (D) they have

322. At this point, the writer is considering adding the following true statement:

    Tides are caused by the gravitational forces of the sun and moon.

    Should the writer make this addition here?
    (A) Yes, because it informs the reader as to the cause of tides.
    (B) Yes, because it reinforces in the reader's mind that the writer is knowledgeable.
    (C) No, because it contradicts what the writer states in the rest of the paragraph.
    (D) No, because it distracts the reader from the main focus of the passage.

323. The best placement for the underlined portion would be
    (A) where it is now.
    (B) before the word *called*.
    (C) after the word *land* (before the period).
    (D) before the word *The*.

324. (A) NO CHANGE
    (B) shifting
    (C) to shift
    (D) having shifted

325. (A) NO CHANGE
    (B) hour—however,
    (C) hour, however,
    (D) hour, however.

326. (A) NO CHANGE
    (B) shallower
    (C) most shallowest
    (D) shallow

327. (A) NO CHANGE
    (B) exposed
    (C) expose
    (D) exposing

328. (A) NO CHANGE
    (B) send out
    (C) did send out
    (D) sends out

329. (A) NO CHANGE
(B) its been
(C) it been
(D) it be

330. For the sake of the logic and coherence of the essay, Paragraph 2 should be placed
(A) where it is now.
(B) after Paragraph 4.
(C) after Paragraph 3.
(D) before Paragraph 1.

Determining Personality Types

A noted thinker, named Joseph Campbell gave some excellent and
—————————————
331
thought-provoking advice about choosing a career. 332 Campbell said, "Follow your bliss." By this he meant that you should let your most deepest interests
—————————
333
and needs lead you to a career that you will enjoy. It may be difficult to decide which career for a young person about to graduate from high school will make
—————————————————————————————
334
one's life happy and productive. Career choice can be hard. But most experts
————
335
in the field of career counseling agree that the most important step you can take is to find a career that suits to your personality.
—————————
336
According to psychologist John Holland, there are six basic personality types that match most people, the six types are the realistic, the investigative, the
—————————
337
artistic: the social, the enterprising, and the conventional. The realistic
————
338
personality is often interested in machines and how they work. This kind of person is suited to such skilled trades as machine and as computer repairman,
——
339
auto mechanic, and electrician. Investigative people enjoy research in science and other fields. Artistic people can be creative in a variety of jobs, such as interior design, illustration, and clothes design. Social people have a strong need to help others and make good social workers, teachers, and counselors. Enterprising

people love adventure and challenges; they often start their own businesses and prefer to be managers and bosses. Conventional people feel most comfortable in a job in which they know exactly what is expected of them. ⃞340 Jobs that suit them include <u>clerical work accounting</u>, and banking. People in the military are

₃₄₁

often both realistic and conventional.

[1] Many careers also call for a combination of personality traits. [2] You can find out which type describes your personality by taking the Vocational Preferences Inventory, a test invented by Holland. [3] <u>However,</u> many people

₃₄₂

find that they have elements of two or more of these personality types. [4] For example, a psychologist who treats patients' problems needs to be investigative (research-oriented). [5] <u>As well as</u> social (wanting to help others). [6] A writer

₃₄₃

who works in advertising might be both artistic and enterprising, or business-oriented. ⃞344

331. (A) NO CHANGE
    (B) noted thinker named
    (C) noted, thinker, named
    (D) noted thinker; named

332. If the writer were to delete the words *excellent* and *thought-provoking* from the preceding sentence, the passage would primarily lose
    (A) what the writer's opinion is of Joseph Campbell's advice.
    (B) why Joseph Campbell talked about career choice.
    (C) the reason why Joseph Campbell became a noted thinker.
    (D) the idea that young people are troubled.

333. (A) NO CHANGE
    (B) deeper
    (C) most deeper
    (D) deepest

334. The best placement for the underlined portion would be

    (A) where it is now.

    (B) after the word *difficult*.

    (C) after the word *decide*.

    (D) after the word *happy*.

335. Which choice best emphasizes the problems of career choice for young people?

    (A) NO CHANGE

    (B) most stressful

    (C) confusing

    (D) uncomfortable

336. (A) NO CHANGE

    (B) suited your

    (C) suited to your

    (D) suits your

337. (A) NO CHANGE

    (B) people: the

    (C) people. The

    (D) people, the

338. (A) NO CHANGE

    (B) the artistic. The

    (C) the artistic; the

    (D) the artistic, the

339. (A) NO CHANGE

    (B) as,

    (C) yet

    (D) OMIT the underlined portion.

340. The writer is considering adding the following sentence here:

They have a strong need for order and rules.

Should the writer include the sentence?

(A) Yes, because it tells more about conventional people.
(B) Yes, because it helps the reader understand what conventional people do.
(C) No, because it contradicts what the rest of the essay says about personality types.
(D) No, because it distracts from the overall message of the essay.

341. (A) NO CHANGE
(B) clerical, work accounting
(C) clerical, work, accounting
(D) clerical work, accounting

342. (A) NO CHANGE
(B) Although
(C) In spite of
(D) OMIT the underlined portion.

343. (A) NO CHANGE
(B) (research-oriented): as well as
(C) (research-oriented), as well as
(D) (research-oriented) as well as

344. For the sake of the logic and coherence of the paragraph, Sentence 1 should be placed

(A) where it is now.
(B) after Sentence 3.
(C) after Sentence 5.
(D) after Sentence 6.

345. Suppose that the writer had set out to write a brief essay on the age at which people should decide which aspect of a career is most important to them. Has the writer been successful at his goal?

(A) Yes, because the essay addresses the problems that young people have in choosing a career.
(B) Yes, because the essay talks about the different personality types.
(C) No, because the essay doesn't talk about the various aspects of a career, only personality types.
(D) No, because the essay doesn't go into detail about which people are good at which jobs.

Remembering Sherbro Island

Note: The following paragraphs may not be in the most logical order. Each paragraph is numbered; question 359 asks you to choose where Paragraph 2 would most logically be placed.

[1] Bonthe was a <u>day's travel</u> by lorry from Joru, the town that I lived in.
      346
I was excited to see the island, because my friend had told me that there were

no cars and everyone walked to their destinations. It turned out to be very

picaresque, with houses that were unusual <u>because they were built on stilts.</u>
                                                        347
I guess it flooded a lot. I remember too the wonderful beaches there.

[2] Sherbro Island is located in the Atlantic Ocean, off the coast of

West Africa. The primary town is the port of Bonthe. It is accessible from the

mainland at Mattru Jong by ferry along the Jong River. Sherbro Island is part

of <u>the country that is called</u> Sierra Leone and was its first capital, when it was
     348
settled by the British toward the end of the eighteenth century. I learned about

Sherbro Island from another volunteer who was stationed there when I was in

the Peace Corps, teaching English as a Second Language. I decided to visit him

and see the island.

[3] Twenty years later, I decided I would return to Sierra Leone to see what

had changed. A <u>problem in the country</u> had prevented me from going earlier.
        349
I knew it would be a nostalgic trip for me. ⌷350⌷ Bonthe would be my first stop

of a ten-day trip.

[4] I had decided to forgo public transportation on my trip, and bravely

rented a car in <u>Freetown they drive</u> on the wrong side of the road there, so
                 351
it would be a challenge. After two hours, I turned off the main road onto

a secondary road that was unpaved, rough, and uncared for. Sections were still eroded from rainy season. From Koribundu to Mattru Jong, the road was even worse, but I got through. I was glad I <u>had chose</u> the four-wheel-drive upgrade.

352

[5] The ferry was <u>crowded with everything</u>, but the 40-minute ride was

353

peaceful; the mangrove swamps were just as I remembered. The sound of the birds in the jungle was cacophonous and mysterious. We all piled off the boat in Bonthe. I asked directions for Bonthe Holiday Village, a resort that wasn't there the last time I had come, but <u>that I had been reading about.</u> The rooms

354

were small, but clean. After a delicious feast of groundnut stew, I slept deeply.

[6] The next day, I walked through the sleepy town. 355 It hadn't changed after all these years. Barefoot children ran and played in the sandy streets. Women leaned <u>stirring fragrant fish stews</u> over big iron pots. The fishermen had

356

all gone out to sea. The Anglican church was still there, looking as dilapidated as it had before. I walked out to Peninsular Beach. It was all just as I remembered, mile after mile of pure white sand, palm trees, crystal clear water. There wasn't another soul on the beach.

[7] Far out at sea I could see the fishermen casting their nets. <u>However,</u> I was

357

glad I had come. Lying on the sand, looking up at the cloudless dry-season sky, I tapped into all the memories of my life as it was so long ago when I first visited the island. Tomorrow I would drive to <u>Joru but</u> now I was going for a swim. 359

358

346. (A) NO CHANGE
    (B) days travel
    (C) days' travel
    (D) day travel

347. (A) NO CHANGE
    (B) because they used stilts to put their houses on
    (C) because the houses stood on stilts in the ground
    (D) OMIT the underlined portion.

348. (A) NO CHANGE
    (B) the country that people know as
    (C) the country known today as
    (D) OMIT the underlined portion.

349. Given that all of the choices are true, which one provides the most significant new information?
    (A) NO CHANGE
    (B) difficulty in the country
    (C) situation that could not be resolved
    (D) long and dangerous civil war

350. If the word *nostalgic* were deleted from the preceding sentence, the essay would primarily lose
    (A) the fact that he wants to reenlist in the Peace Corps.
    (B) why the writer waited so long to take the trip.
    (C) the reason for going to Bonthe.
    (D) an idea of what the writer feels about his trip.

351. (A) NO CHANGE
    (B) Freetown. They
    (C) Freetown, they
    (D) Freetown—they

352. (A) NO CHANGE
    (B) was chosen
    (C) has chosen
    (D) had chosen

353. Given that all of the choices are true, which one provides the most significant additional information?
    (A) NO CHANGE
    (B) filled with people, chickens, and children
    (C) had a lot of people
    (D) filled to capacity

354. (A) NO CHANGE
    (B) that I read about
    (C) that I had read about earlier
    (D) OMIT the underlined portion.

355. If the word *sleepy* were deleted from the preceding sentence, the essay would primarily lose

(A) an idea of what the town was like.

(B) the sense that the writer was tired.

(C) the suggestion that residents often napped during the day.

(D) the idea that people did not walk around much.

356. The best placement for the underlined portion would be

(A) where it is now.

(B) after the word *Women.*

(C) after the word *over.*

(D) after the word *pots.*

357. (A) NO CHANGE

(B) Yet,

(C) Moreover,

(D) OMIT the underlined portion.

358. (A) NO CHANGE

(B) Joru, but

(C) Joru—but

(D) Joru: but

359. For the sake of the logic and coherence of the essay, Paragraph 2 should be placed

(A) where it is now.

(B) before Paragraph 1.

(C) after Paragraph 3.

(D) after Paragraph 4.

360. Suppose that the writer had wanted to write an essay that captured his feelings about a place that he had visited many years before. Was he successful in doing that?

(A) Yes, because he had the chance to revisit his past and relive his memories.

(B) Yes, because he was able to describe in detail what his life was like while in the Peace Corps.

(C) No, because he failed to tell about his feelings about the past.

(D) No, because the essay was not descriptive enough.

Born to Be a Vet

Its strange, but true, ever since I was little, I knew I been a veterinarian when
361　　　　362　　　　　　　　　363
I grew up. I just loved animals. I grew up on a small farm in Minnesota, and

I like to watch as the vet treated a sick cow that wouldn't get up. The vet gave the
364
cow an IV saline solution, before the bag was empty and the cow would rise right
365
up. My parents had 34 dairy cows, but there were also lots of chickens and geese.

We had three dogs and four cats and two horses too. When I was five, my father

let me help milk the cows.

I helped him every day until I started going to school. My parents' farm was

way out in the country and the school bus picked me up at 6:30 in the morning,

since our house was first on the route. When I was in high school, I volunteered
366
at the local humane society. I cleaned the dirtier cages and washed blankets.
367
I learned how to groom. I took the dogs for walks and played with the cats.

I stuffed envelopes with brochures about being a foster parent for young puppies

and kittens. On weekends, I went to the local mall with dogs and cats who
368
needed homes that would provide affection and love, and talked to people,

encouraging them to adopt a pet because they needed love. 369

After graduating from high school, I was fortunate to receive a scholarship

at State. I found that I possess a natural flair for science, and I enrolled in Biology
370
and Chemistry classes. After my first year, I decided to major in Biology. That

summer, I found a local animal hospital where I could intern. I learned how to

perform lab tests, and the technicians taught me how to use the equipment and

interpret the test results. Whenever I could find the time, I returned home to the

farm, I was an only child, and my parents were always overjoyed to see me.
371

[1] I was worried that it would be difficult for me to get in, because I was female and from a small midwestern farming community. [2] During my senior year, I decided to apply to a Veterinary Medicine graduate school. [3] However, <u>372</u> I was surprised when I talked to one of the deans to hear that that <u>years</u> <u>373</u> graduating class was 82% female. [4] So <u>I crossed</u> my fingers and sent in my <u>374</u> application. [5] A month later, I received my acceptance letter. [6] In four years I would become a Doctor of Veterinary Medicine. [375]

It was difficult, but it happened. I opened a practice in my hometown, where I have so many friends and wonderful memories, and I couldn't be happier in my work.

361. (A) NO CHANGE
     (B) Its'
     (C) It's
     (D) They're

362. (A) NO CHANGE
     (B) true. Ever
     (C) true ever
     (D) true . . . ever

363. (A) NO CHANGE
     (B) I have been
     (C) I will be
     (D) I would be

364. (A) NO CHANGE
     (B) liked to watch
     (C) liked to have watched
     (D) liked to be watching

365. The best placement for the underlined portion would be
     (A) where it is now.
     (B) before the word *would*.
     (C) after the word *vet*.
     (D) after the word *up*.

366. Given that all of the choices are true, which one provides the most significant new information?

(A) NO CHANGE
(B) which was very early.
(C) so I couldn't help.
(D) and the driver always smiled.

367. (A) NO CHANGE
(B) more dirty
(C) dirty
(D) dirtiest

368. (A) NO CHANGE
(B) whom
(C) that
(D) OMIT the underlined portion.

369. If the writer were to delete the phrase "because they needed love" from the preceding sentence, the sentence would primarily lose

(A) the idea that the pets need affection.
(B) a description of what pets need.
(C) an indication that the writer loves pets.
(D) nothing, because the phrase is redundant.

370. (A) NO CHANGE
(B) possessed
(C) possessing
(D) to possess

371. (A) NO CHANGE
(B) farm. I
(C) farm I
(D) farm: I

372. Which of the following alternatives to the underlined portion would NOT be acceptable?

(A) Yet
(B) Consequently
(C) Still
(D) Nevertheless

373. (A) NO CHANGE
    (B) year
    (C) years'
    (D) year's

374. (A) NO CHANGE
    (B) I cross
    (C) I was crossing
    (D) I had crossed

375. For the sake of the logic and coherence of the paragraph, Sentence 2 should be

    (A) placed where it is now.
    (B) placed before Sentence 1.
    (C) placed before Sentence 4.
    (D) OMITTED from the paragraph.

CHAPTER 6

Set 2 English Questions

The Aviatrix

Amelia Earhart, born in 1897 in Atchison, <u>Kansas was</u> a pioneer in the
376
early days of aviation. Called "the Lady of the Air," she was a role model

to women all around the world. <u>However,</u> Amelia was the first woman, and
377
the second person after Charles Lindbergh, to fly solo across the Atlantic

Ocean in 1932, and the first woman to fly alone from Hawaii to California

in 1935. At a time when men dominated aviation, she was truly a celebrated

aviatrix. 378

In 1937, Amelia <u>decides</u> she wanted to be the first person to fly
379
around the world at the equator, a distance totaling 29,000 miles.

<u>Funding from Purdue University</u>, she outfitted a twin-engine Lockheed
380
Electra <u>with oversized fuel tanks and special radio equipment</u>. This was
381
before radar had been invented, so she would have to rely on radio

communication for direction. Realizing she would need <u>help, she</u> recruited
382
Fred Noonan, an experienced navigator who <u>was charting</u> air routes across
383
the Pacific for the fledgling commercial airline industry.

[1] Earhart and Noonan set out on their trip on June 1, 1937, departing

from Miami, Florida. [2] They made <u>its</u> way eastward and, by early July,
384

they had reached New Guinea, having flown 22,000 miles. [3] On July 2, they took off from Lae Airport. [4] They had a distance of over 2,500 miles to get to Howland Island, a tiny uninhabited island <u>which</u> the U.S. government had built
385
an airfield and fuel tanks for her. [5] The U.S. Coast Guard had stationed the cutter *Itasca* by the island to maintain radio contact with the plane. [6] Despite a massive search-and-rescue operation that covered 250,000 square miles, no trace was ever found of the plane or its crew. [7] Their plane, <u>though,</u> was having
386
difficulty maintaining radio contact with the *Itasca*; transmissions were faint and broken by static. [8] At 8:45 that morning, Amelia radioed, "We are running north and south." [9] Those were her last words. 387

Many people have put forth theories of Amelia's disappearance and conducted searches, all to no avail <u>over the years.</u> In August, 2012, a search team
388
using a remote operating vehicle (ROV) took pictures of what is purported to be part of a wheel assembly: a strut, wheel, gear, and fender, found far below the surface of the sea near Nikumaroro Island, a tiny atoll of less than two square miles, located 400 miles southwest of Howland Island. The next step would be to send an unmanned submarine to retrieve the <u>parts then</u> see if they do indeed
389
belong to a Lockheed Electra, but that has not happened. Possibly one day, we will all find out what <u>was happening</u> to Amelia Earhart and Fred Noonan. 391
390

376. (A) NO CHANGE
   (B) Kansas, was
   (C) Kansas: was
   (D) Kansas; was

377. (A) NO CHANGE
   (B) While
   (C) Although
   (D) OMIT the underlined portion.

378. The writer is considering revising the first part of this sentence ("At a time when men dominated aviation,") to read as follows:

> At a time when flying was new,

If the writer did this, the essay would primarily lose

(A) an indication that planes were not very safe at the time.
(B) a detail that helps the reader understand how special Amelia Earhart was.
(C) a detail that gives the reader more information about how popular aviation was at the time.
(D) a possibly confusing issue over what aviation was like at the time.

379. (A) NO CHANGE
(B) deciding
(C) has decided
(D) decided

380. (A) NO CHANGE
(B) With funding from Purdue University
(C) After funds were given by Purdue University
(D) With funds that came from a university called Purdue

381. (A) NO CHANGE
(B) oversized fuel tanks and special radio equipment
(C) having oversized fuel tanks and special radio equipment
(D) OMIT the underlined portion.

382. (A) NO CHANGE
(B) help; she
(C) help she
(D) help. She

383. (A) NO CHANGE
(B) charting
(C) charted
(D) charts

384. (A) NO CHANGE
(B) his
(C) her
(D) their

385. (A) NO CHANGE
    (B) that
    (C) where
    (D) OMIT the underlined portion.

386. Which of the following alternatives to the underlined portion would NOT be acceptable?
    (A) however
    (B) since
    (C) nonetheless
    (D) nevertheless

387. For the sake of the logic and coherence of the paragraph, Sentence 6 should be placed
    (A) where it is now.
    (B) after Sentence 1.
    (C) after Sentence 9.
    (D) OMITTED from the paragraph.

388. The best placement for the underlined portion would be
    (A) where it is now.
    (B) after the word *people.*
    (C) after the word *disappearance.*
    (D) after the word *searches.*

389. (A) NO CHANGE
    (B) parts and then
    (C) parts, then
    (D) parts and, then

390. (A) NO CHANGE
    (B) have happened
    (C) were happening
    (D) happened

391. At this point, the writer is considering adding the following true statement:

> Noonan joined the Merchant Marine in 1906.

Should the writer make this addition here?

(A) Yes, because it provides further details about Noonan before he was lost.

(B) Yes, because it strengthens the idea that Noonan was a resourceful person.

(C) No, because it has no bearing on what the passage is mostly about.

(D) No, because it creates confusion about what Noonan was like.

History of Advertising

Note: The following paragraphs may not be in the most logical order. Each paragraph is numbered; question 406 asks you to choose where Paragraph 4 would most logically be placed.

[1] It is thought commonly that merchants did not advertise before the
<u>392</u>
twentieth century, but the truth is that people were advertising for hundreds

of years before that. In the Middle Ages, European merchants returned from the

Orient with silk and spices that had <u>never been ever seen before.</u> <u>Instead of</u>
                              393   394

peddling their goods from door to door, they hired a man to run through the

streets of the city shouting that exotic silks and spices from the East could be

bought. 395 The man who ran through the streets was called a "crier."

[2] Very few people could read then, so advertising was done exclusively by

criers for many years. <u>Later, merchants'</u> painted signs for the front of their shops.
                396

But instead of <u>words, they</u> used pictures of their merchandise. The invention
               397

of the printing press in the fifteenth century meant that more people learned

to read. <u>Nevertheless,</u> printed posters became more commonplace advertising
     398

tools. The first newspaper ad was published in <u>1704, the</u> *Boston News-Letter* ran
                 399

an ad for a house for sale in Oyster Bay, Long Island. In 1742, Benjamin

Franklin published *The General Magazine and Historical Chronicle for all the British Plantations in America* with the first magazine ads. The first advertising agency opened in Philadelphia in 1843.

[3] Today, television dominates the advertising world, with total revenues in 2011 of $190 billion. 400 Internet ad sales are growing by leaps and bounds. Magazine and newspaper advertising has declining, especially with the advent
401
of tablet computers and e-readers, as more and more people prefer reading on electronic devices. 402 Although the methods may have changed and more likely
403
will continue to change, advertising one's products is certainly here to stay.

[4] In 1922, a New York City radio station, WEAF (which later became WNBC) broadcast the first advertisement on radio, promoting a new apartment complex in Jackson Heights. 404 And in 1941, as well in New York City, the first
405
television broadcast aired on July 1. At this time, advertising cost $120 an hour for an evening show. Compare that to the average network cost in 2011 for a "prime-time" 30-second slot of $110,000. With the advent of the Internet in the 1990s, another advertising avenue opened. 406

392. The best placement for the underlined portion would be
  (A) where it is now.
  (B) after the word *is.*
  (C) after the word *merchants.*
  (D) after the word *advertise.*

393. (A) NO CHANGE
  (B) never ever seen before
  (C) never been seen before
  (D) never seen before

394. (A) NO CHANGE
  (B) While
  (C) In spite of
  (D) OMIT the underlined portion.

395. If the writer were to delete the word *exotic* and the phrase "from the East" from the preceding sentence, the sentence would primarily lose

    (A) the reasoning behind the use of a crier.

    (B) the suggestion that the items were not easily obtained.

    (C) the idea that Eastern silks and spices were commonplace.

    (D) a comparison between the silk and the spices.

396. (A) NO CHANGE

    (B) Later merchants'

    (C) Later, merchant's

    (D) Later, merchants

397. (A) NO CHANGE

    (B) words they

    (C) words. They

    (D) words; they

398. (A) NO CHANGE

    (B) Consequently,

    (C) However,

    (D) OMIT the underlined portion.

399. (A) NO CHANGE

    (B) 1704. The

    (C) 1704 the

    (D) 1704—the

400. The writer is considering revising the preceding sentence to read as follows:

    Nowadays, television gets a great deal of revenue from advertising.

If the writer does this, the essay would primarily lose

    (A) a feeling for which kind of advertising is the most lucrative.

    (B) an actual idea of the amount of money that is spent on television advertising.

    (C) the idea that television advertising might be replaced by Internet advertising.

    (D) the concept that political advertising is increasing.

401. (A) NO CHANGE

    (B) have declining

    (C) been declining

    (D) has declined

402. If the writer were to delete the phrase "especially with the advent of tablet computers and e-readers" from the preceding sentence, the sentence would primarily lose

    (A) the reason why magazine and newspaper advertising revenues have declined.

    (B) an awareness of why people prefer tablet computers and e-readers.

    (C) a knowledge of how much revenue has been lost by magazines and newspapers.

    (D) the idea that people are whimsical when it comes to watching advertisements.

403. (A) NO CHANGE
    (B) much likely
    (C) likelier
    (D) most likely

404. At this point, the writer is considering adding the following true statement:

> Jackson Heights is a community in Queens, one of New York City's six boroughs, and is known for its garden apartment buildings.

Should the writer make this addition here?

    (A) Yes, because it informs the reader about what Jackson Heights is known for.

    (B) Yes, because it informs the reader that the writer knows how many boroughs there are in New York City.

    (C) No, because the information does not fit in with the main focus of the paragraph, which is about how advertising evolved.

    (D) No, because the reader could be confused by the information about how many boroughs there are in New York City.

405. (A) NO CHANGE
    (B) too
    (C) also
    (D) OMIT the underlined portion.

406. For the sake of the logic and coherence of the essay, Paragraph 4 should be placed

    (A) where it is now.
    (B) before Paragraph 1.
    (C) before Paragraph 2.
    (D) before Paragraph 3.

407. Suppose the writer had intended to write a brief essay showing how important advertising has been throughout history. Would this essay successfully fulfill the writer's goal?

   (A) Yes, because the essay shows how integral advertising has been since early times when someone wanted to sell something.

   (B) Yes, because the essay shows how much income was made from advertising in the past and in modern times.

   (C) No, because the focus of the essay is on income rather than the history of advertising.

   (D) No, because the essay fails to cover fully why advertising came into existence.

The Sioux Nation

South Dakota was the home of the great Sioux Nation. In all, there were about 20,000 Sioux in three groups, the Lakota, Dakota, and <u>Nakota comprising</u>
₄₀₈
14 different tribes throughout the Great Plains. They were nomads riding the plains on horses that were brought to this country by the Spanish conquistador Hernan Cortés in 1519. The horses were a great help to the Sioux as they traveled about hunting the buffalo. <u>By using these horses,</u> they could easily transport
₄₀₉
their teepees and equipment from place to place.

The Sioux people were their own masters, <u>not having rules.</u> Their lives
₄₁₀
were based on hunting, gathering <u>foodstuffs; and caring</u> for their young.
₄₁₁
Children were considered special and were called *wakanisha*, or sacred ones. The Sioux passed down to their children the stories that were the foundation of their civilization. Their central belief was the principle of living in harmony with nature and the environment. The area known as the Black Hills was considered holy ground. Through their relationship with nature,

<u>and particularly the animals they hunted,</u> the Sioux developed a unique
₄₁₂
and sophisticated culture.

[1] Their connection with nature is most evident in stories that have handed
$\underline{}$
413

down generation after generation, and that are still told on the reservations today.

[2] These stories are meant to explain the origins of the world and the Sioux's

relationship to these origins. [3] A typical story tells how the rainbow came to be.
$\underline{}$
414

[4] It was said to be made from colorful summer flowers that die in the fall.

[5] The young artist ran out of paint, so the loons are gray, as the story

goes. [6] Another explains why ducks have so many different-colored feathers.

[7] An Indian brave painted them and each one is, consequent, different.
$\underline{}$
415

[8] Many of their stories are about the buffalo, which was an important part
$\underline{}$
416

of their lives and culture. [9] The buffalo provided them with everything from

food to clothing to housing. [10] It was also the basis of many of the Sioux's

myths and legends. 417

During the mid-1800s, the culture of the Sioux, which was nomadic and

centered on the buffalo and the horse, increasingly conflicted with the culture

of the white man, which was industrial and agricultural based. Tensions flared
$\underline{}$
418

when gold was discovered in the Black Hills in 1874 by an expedition led by

George Custer. The U.S. government offered the Sioux $6 million for the

Black Hills, which was refused. A series of battles ensued, concomitant
$\underline{}$
419

in the Battle of the Little Bighorn in Greasy Grass, Montana. On June 25,

1876, General Custer and over 200 soldiers of the 7th U.S. Army Cavalry

Regiment perished fighting the Sioux, led by their famous chief, Sitting Bull,
$\underline{}$
420

and their allies, the Cheyenne. The victory was short-lived, however, as other

soldiers invaded the hunting grounds of the Sioux. Within five years, all the

Sioux and Cheyenne would be restricted to living on reservations.

Today the Sioux has a renewed sense of pride. Children are taught
                    <u>421</u>
their <u>native</u> customs and language. Native American artists produce buffalo
      <u>422</u>
hide paintings, beadwork, and pottery. In 2012, over $9 million was raised by

Hollywood stars and musicians, and the revered and sacred site of Pe' Sla in the

Black Hills was reacquired. ⟨423⟩ The great Sioux Nation can once again host

annual ceremonies at the site that is central to the Lakota Creation Myth.

408. (A) NO CHANGE
    (B) Nakota, comprising
    (C) Nakota, comprised
    (D) Nakota,

409. (A) NO CHANGE
    (B) These horses,
    (C) In using these horses,
    (D) With these horses,

410. Given that all of the choices are true, which one provides the most
significant new information?
    (A) NO CHANGE
    (B) without any restraints on them.
    (C) roaming freely as they pleased.
    (D) with no place to call home.

411. (A) NO CHANGE
    (B) foodstuffs. And caring
    (C) foodstuffs, and caring
    (D) foodstuffs and caring

412. (A) NO CHANGE
    (B) and particularly the animals they hunt,
    (C) in particularly the animals they hunted,
    (D) and particularly with the animals they hunted,

413. (A) NO CHANGE
    (B) have been handed
    (C) were being handed
    (D) are being handed

414. (A) NO CHANGE
     (B) comes to be
     (C) came to have been
     (D) came to being

415. (A) NO CHANGE
     (B) consequently,
     (C) consequencely,
     (D) with consequence,

416. (A) NO CHANGE
     (B) an integral part
     (C) a big part
     (D) an occurring part

417. For the sake of logic and coherence of the paragraph, Sentence 5 should be placed
     (A) where it is now.
     (B) before Sentence 2.
     (C) after Sentence 3.
     (D) after Sentence 7.

418. (A) NO CHANGE
     (B) industry and agricultural base
     (C) industrially and agriculturally based
     (D) based on industry and agriculture

419. (A) NO CHANGE
     (B) culminating
     (C) cascading
     (D) collaterally

420. The best placement for the underlined phrase would be
     (A) where it is now.
     (B) after the word *Regiment.*
     (C) at the beginning of the sentence.
     (D) after the word *soldiers.*

421. (A) NO CHANGE
     (B) had
     (C) have
     (D) are having

422. (A) NO CHANGE
(B) the native
(C) the natives'
(D) native

423. At this point, the writer is considering adding the following true statement:

> Pe' Sla was considered to be "The Heart of Everything That Is" by the Sioux.

Should the writer make this addition here?

(A) Yes, because it informs the reader how the Sioux feel about Pe' Sla.
(B) Yes, because it shows the reader that the writer did a lot of research.
(C) No, because it distracts the reader from the main focus of the paragraph.
(D) No, because it contradicts the writer's statement in the following sentence.

A Memory of Marco and Polo

Note: The following paragraphs may not be in the most logical order. Each paragraph is numbered; question 438 asks you to choose where Paragraph 3 would most logically be placed.

[1] One sunny and hot afternoon in July when I was 12, I <u>played</u> in the

₄₂₄

backyard of our house, when I spotted two small turtles slowly walking through

the <u>grass, they</u> were about an inch or so across. They had a hard shell that was

₄₂₅

green with little yellow stripes. Excitedly, I ran into the house to tell my

mother. 426 We came out a few minutes later and found the turtles lounging

on some rocks by our garden. They were clearly sunning themselves.

[2] My mom looked the turtles up on her computer. <u>From their markings,</u>

₄₂₇

it <u>appeared</u> they belonged to a species of turtle called the river cooter.

₄₂₇

The species <u>accesses</u> rivers and wetlands, and since our house was less

₄₂₈

than a half mile from the Satilla River, that <u>must being</u> where they

₄₂₉

had come from. We read that cooters often could be domesticated as pets

as long as you had an aquatic environment to support them. Since we had
<u>   </u>
430

an aquarium in our house, I begged my mom to let us keep them. She agreed,

on the condition that I am responsible for taking care of them. I carefully picked
                                                431

the turtles up and carried them to the aquarium.

[3] We had a 100-gallon fish tank in the house. My mother was really into

fish. She had neon tetras and knife fish, but her favorite were two red bettas.

Lifting up the lid, I gently slipped the turtles into the warm water. They seemed

happy and quickly start swimming around. They didn't chase the fish and the
                                       432

fish didn't seem to mind the turtles. I read some more about my river cooters.

I learned that they were herbivorous, which means they ate plants. 433 I took

some lettuce from the refrigerator and cut it into little pieces. They were clearly

hungry and gobbled it all up.

[4] I named my turtles Marco and Polo. Since I didn't know if they were

male or female, I decided on the names from my favorite swimming pool game.

I went to the pet store and got turtle food. I made a basking area out of some

bark and floated it on the surface of the water. They loved laying under the heat
                                             434

lamp. As the summer wore on, Marco and Polo grew, and little pieces of their

carapace, or shell, would come off and new shell would replace it.

[5] School began again. I came home every day and fed the turtles. They were

growing very fast, almost three inches in diameter. I read that the river cooter
                                   435

could measure as much as 13 inches across as an adult. They were becoming
                                                    436

much too big, even for our enormous fish tank. I went to my mom and we

discussed the future for Marco and Polo. There was only one thing to do.

Together we put my turtles into a shoebox and walked down to the edge of the river. I put them on a rock. They seemed to look back at me and then quietly slipped into the water. I was a little sad after that, but I knew it was best for them. One night a few months later, I had a dream. I dreamt that Marco was pregnant. She would have a baby turtle in the spring and she thanked me for taking care of her and Polo. I felt proud that I had helped them. 438

437

424. (A) NO CHANGE
   (B) did play
   (C) was playing
   (D) could play

425. (A) NO CHANGE
   (B) grass—they
   (C) grass they
   (D) grass. They

426. If the word *excitedly* were deleted from the previous sentence, the essay would primarily lose
   (A) a suggestion that the writer was afraid.
   (B) a detail that changes the meaning of the sentence.
   (C) evidence that the writer did not like the turtles.
   (D) support for the previous sentence.

427. (A) NO CHANGE
   (B) From their markings, it appears
   (C) It appears, from their markings
   (D) From their markings it appeared

428. (A) NO CHANGE
   (B) claims
   (C) inhabits
   (D) dominates

429. (A) NO CHANGE
   (B) must have was
   (C) must have been
   (D) must been

430. The best placement for the underlined phrase is
  (A) where it is now.
  (B) after the word *them.*
  (C) after the word *domesticated.*
  (D) before the word *We.*

431. (A) NO CHANGE
  (B) would be responsible
  (C) are responsible
  (D) was responsible

432. (A) NO CHANGE
  (B) start to swim
  (C) started swimming
  (D) starts swimming

433. At this point, the writer is considering adding the following true statement:

   I also read that young turtles love to eat fresh lettuce.

Should the writer make this addition here?
  (A) Yes, because it tells what kind of plant turtles will eat.
  (B) Yes, because it informs the reader that the writer needed to cut the lettuce up.
  (C) No, because the writer previously stated that the turtles ate plants.
  (D) No, because it distracts the reader and doesn't fit logically in the passage.

434. (A) NO CHANGE
  (B) lain
  (C) lying
  (D) to lay

435. (A) NO CHANGE
  (B) very fast, nearly three inches in diameter.
  (C) very fast. They were nearly three inches in diameter.
  (D) very fast, but they were nearly three inches in diameter.

436. (A) NO CHANGE
  (B) would become
  (C) would have become
  (D) would be becoming

437. Which of the following choices best emphasizes how the writer responded to letting the turtles go free?
   (A) NO CHANGE
   (B) I felt a little funny.
   (C) It was odd at first.
   (D) It wasn't so bad after that.

438. For the sake of the logic and coherence of the essay, Paragraph 3 should be placed
   (A) where it is now.
   (B) before Paragraph 1.
   (C) before Paragraph 2.
   (D) after Paragraph 4.

439. Suppose that the writer had intended to write a brief essay about a child's learning to accept the fact that life is often full of change. Would this essay successfully fulfill that goal?
   (A) Yes, because the essay shows that the writer felt that the mother was a good parent.
   (B) Yes, because the essay shows that the writer accepted the loss of the turtles by having a positive dream.
   (C) No, because the focus of the essay was primarily on river cooters.
   (D) No, because the essay was not about change, but a summer in the life of a young boy.

Superman

During all of time, people have enjoyed myths about heroes with amazing
  440
powers. The ancient Greeks had Hercules with his mighty strength. The Middle

Ages produced Beowulf, a fearless warrior who defeated the monster Grendel.

Paul Bunyan was a giant lumberjack in early American folklore who

becomes a symbol of might. But the superhero to end all superheroes was
  441
Superman. The comic book hero Superman was created by two imaginative

17-year-olds named Jerry Siegel and Joe Shuster in 1933. 442 He was the first

superhero. With his special powers, he was able to fight any evildoers. Originally,
  443

Superman couldn't fly, but he could leap an eighth of a mile at a time. That was fast enough to catch a criminal. He had X-ray vision and supersharp hearing, which were excellent tools for tracking down criminals. As time went on, he was
_____
444
given more powers, including the ability to fly. He could travel through time at the speed of light. By the end of World War II, Superman would even survive
_____
445
a nuclear blast unharmed. In fact, Superman took the identity of mild-mannered
_____   _____
446   447
newspaper reporter Clark Kent. Ordinary people saw themselves in Clark Kent. They saw injustice and suffering all around them and felt helpless about it.

But when Clark Kent took off his tie and business shirt so as to reveal the
_____
448
blue-and-red-caped uniform of Superman, every reader felt a thrill. This was the perfect way for ordinary people to feel powerful. They could feel since they were
_____
449
Superman, fighting for the innocent and prostrate against the villains of the
_____
450
world. As Superman said, "There is a right and a wrong in the universe and that distinction is not hard to make."*

Americans weren't the only ones to follow the adventures of the Man of Steel. Superman became popular all around the world. From his origin as a comic book hero, Superman moved on to radio and then television and movies. ⎡451⎤ He can be found in cartoons and computer games. His adventures have been recorded on audiotapes and DVDs. Why has Superman stayed popular for nearly 80 years? Other action heroes have come and gone, but Superman has remained a favorite.
_____
452
Some people think the reason is that Superman seemingly cares about people.
_____   _____
453   454
He wants to protect ordinary people against evil. To many Americans, Superman stands for the values and beliefs that Americans care about. Superman represents "truth, justice, and the American way."
_____
455

_____

Superman: Last Son of Krypton by Elliot S. Maggin (New York: Warner Books, 1978).

440. (A) NO CHANGE
(B) In time
(C) Throughout time
(D) All along time

441. (A) NO CHANGE
(B) became a symbol
(C) becoming a symbol
(D) is becoming a symbol

442. If the word *imaginative* were deleted from the previous sentence, the essay would primarily lose

(A) a suggestion that Jerry Siegel and Joe Shuster were talented.
(B) evidence that Jerry Siegel and Joe Shuster worked together.
(C) a hint about Superman's nature.
(D) evidence that Superman was created as a joke.

443. Given that all the choices are true, which one best supports the sentence's claims about Superman's powers?

(A) NO CHANGE
(B) he could overcome any problems.
(C) he was better than everyone else.
(D) he had the chance to defend himself.

444. (A) NO CHANGE
(B) which were handy
(C) which could be excellent
(D) OMIT the underlined portion.

445. (A) NO CHANGE
(B) could even survive
(C) could even survives
(D) would have even survived

446. (A) NO CHANGE
(B) For instance
(C) Therefore
(D) OMIT the underlined portion.

447. If the writer were to delete the word *mild-mannered,* the sentence would primarily lose

(A) a comparison between Superman and other superheroes.

(B) a detail that stresses how ordinary people feel about Superman.

(C) the suggestion that Superman and Clark Kent were similar in nature.

(D) a contrast to the powers of Superman.

448. (A) NO CHANGE

(B) to reveal

(C) and revealing

(D) OMIT the underlined portion.

449. (A) NO CHANGE

(B) as if they were

(C) as though they'd be

(D) although they were

450. (A) NO CHANGE

(B) servile

(C) rejected

(D) helpless

451. At this point, the writer is considering adding the following true statement:

The film *Superman Returns* was released to critical acclaim in 2006.

Should the writer make this addition here?

(A) Yes, because it provides an important detail for the paragraph.

(B) Yes, because it reinforces the paragraph's statement that Superman is in movies.

(C) No, because it distracts attention from the paragraph's focus on the different media Superman appears in.

(D) No, because it isn't timely information.

452. Which of the following alternatives to the underlined portion would NOT be acceptable?

(A) besides

(B) nevertheless, preceded by a semicolon instead of a comma and followed by a comma

(C) yet

(D) however, preceded by a semicolon instead of a comma and followed by a comma

453. (A) NO CHANGE
   (B) think why the reason is
   (C) think that is
   (D) think which the reason is

454. (A) NO CHANGE
   (B) apparently
   (C) truly
   (D) OMIT the underlined portion.

455. If the writer were to delete the quotation marks around the phrase "truth, justice, and the American way," the sentence would primarily lose a feature that suggests

   (A) the writer is putting words in Superman's mouth.
   (B) those words are what Superman lives for.
   (C) the words are a direct quote from Superman.
   (D) Superman doesn't believe in those words.

Sojourner Truth

Sojourner Truth was one of the more remarkable women leaders America

<u>456</u>

has produced. Although there are no records of her birth, historians believe that

Sojourner was probably born in 1797 in Ulster County, New York. We do know

that this African-American was born a slave named Isabella Baumfree. She was

sold away from her parents when she was just a child. She took the name

<u>457</u>

Sojourner Truth after she was free by the New York State Emancipation Act

<u>458</u>

of 1827. Her new name represented the ideals, for which she lived and fought.

<u>459</u>

Sojourner moved to New York City, where she began to work with a plethora of

<u>460</u>

organizations that helped women. Later, she became a leading abolitionist who

<u>461</u>

fought against slavery. Fighting for freedom and for equality for women,

Sojourner Truth became a leader in these struggles. In 1850, she published

The Narrative of Sojourner Truth: A Northern Slave. Her book provided a small

income, and she was often invite to speak about anti-slavery and womens rights
                    ——————   ——————————
                      462   463
topics.

Sojourner was a powerful speaker with a quick wit and strong presence.
She drew huge crowds with her speeches. Never intimidated by opposition,
Sojourner Truth was always looking for people of whom she could convince
                                              —————————
                                                464
of the truth. As she once said, "I feel safe in the midst of my enemies, for the
truth is all powerful and will prevail." Her most famous speech, "Ain't I a
woman?", was given in 1851 at a women's rights convention in Ohio. It urged
————————
  465
those at the convention not to ignore the plight of African-American women.

[1] This brave woman challenged injustice wherever she saw them.
                                          —————————————————————
                                                   466
[2] One example was her fight for the desegregation of public transportation
in Washington, D.C. [3] When all the slaves were liberated after the Civil War,
Sojourner worked in the Freedmen's Bureau. [4] One day, Sojourner and a white
woman were walking down the street and became tired. [5] Even though the
Washington streetcars were supposed to integrated, they remained segregated.
                        ———————————————————————
                                 467
[6] Sojourner had her friend hail the trolley, and they both got on.
[7] A conductor grabbed Sojourner and tried to keep her from getting on.
[8] He grabbed her so hard that he injured her shoulder. [9] Sojourner took the
                    ———————————
                        468
trolley company to court and received $125 in damages, a large amount in those
days. [10] This government agency was set up to help former slaves learn skills.
[11] The conductor was fired. [12] The next day, the trolley system was declared
open to all passengers. 469 Sojourner lived a long and productive life and won
much respect and admiration. She even spoke before President Lincoln. Age and
ill health caused her retiring from the lecture circuit. She spent her last days in
                       ———————————
                           470
Battle Creek, Michigan, where she died in 1883.

In 2009, Sojourner Truth became the first African-American woman to have

a bust in the U.S. Capitol. The statue is in Emancipation Hall, named in honor

of all the slaves who worked on the construction of the Capitol.

456. (A) NO CHANGE
  (B) more remarkable woman
  (C) most remarkable women
  (D) OMIT the underlined portion.

457. Given that all the choices are true, which one provides the most significant
  new information?
  (A) NO CHANGE
  (B) when she was young
  (C) while she was still growing
  (D) when she was only nine years old

458. (A) NO CHANGE
  (B) when she was freed
  (C) after she was freed
  (D) after she was freer

459. (A) NO CHANGE
  (B) ideals for which
  (C) ideals: for which
  (D) ideals under which

460. (A) NO CHANGE
  (B) a profusion of
  (C) a scarcity of
  (D) OMIT the underlined portion.

461. (A) NO CHANGE
  (B) would become
  (C) was becoming
  (D) would have become

462. (A) NO CHANGE
  (B) often invited
  (C) was often invited
  (D) was oft invited

463. (A) NO CHANGE
    (B) women's rights
    (C) womens' rights
    (D) women's right

464. (A) NO CHANGE
    (B) of who
    (C) that
    (D) OMIT the underlined portion.

465. (A) NO CHANGE
    (B) woman"?, was
    (C) woman?," was
    (D) woman?" was

466. (A) NO CHANGE
    (B) when she saw them
    (C) whenever she saw that
    (D) whenever she saw it

467. (A) NO CHANGE
    (B) were supposed to been integrated
    (C) were supposed to have been integrated
    (D) were supposed to have been integrate

468. (A) NO CHANGE
    (B) so hardly that
    (C) so harder that
    (D) so much hard that

469. For the sake of the logic and coherence of this paragraph, Sentence 10 should be placed
    (A) where it is now.
    (B) after Sentence 1.
    (C) after Sentence 3.
    (D) before Sentence 6.

470. (A) NO CHANGE
    (B) having retired from
    (C) retired from
    (D) to retire from

On Motherhood

Note: The following paragraphs may not be in the most logical order. Each paragraph is numbered; question 484 asks you to choose where Paragraph 2 would most logically be placed.

[1] Let us consider motherhood. 471 There is no greater joy on Planet Earth. Since there are endless duties to the job, the rewards are numerous. Still, with
472
the fast-paced lifestyle so common today, mothers can feel challenged by external societal factors, like peer pressure and entertainment media. For instance, it is
473
sometimes difficult to be patient. A survey by the Pew Research Center in 2007 finds that 70 percent of adults surveyed said it was harder to be a mother today
474
than it was in the 1970s or 1980s.

[2] When my son called to ask if I could drop off his track uniform for an unscheduled track meet that afternoon, I raced to the school to give it to him and to find out what time he would need to be picked up afterwards.
475
I arrived and asked the secretary if she could call him to the office. Classes were just finishing and the hall were filled with high school students.
476
When my son saw me, his face at once lit up with a huge smile. As he took
477
his uniform and gave me the information about pickup times, he just kept smiling as if we hadn't met in ages 478 and he was really glad to see me. He didn't seem to be embarrassed at all about being there in the high school with all of his friends around talking to his mother. In fact, he seemed quite
479
proud. The harried pace I'd been keeping fell away as I enjoyed this small moment. That smile brightened the rest of my day every time I thought of it.

[3] Sometimes we don't always feel the fruition of being a mother.
480
But I remember one incident that brought to mind how special motherhood is. I been having a very busy day. It was filled with a doctor's appointment,
481

a meeting with my daughter's teacher, mounds of work at the office, deadlines,

and <u>pressure. Plus</u> there was still grocery shopping to be done. Career and
482

motherhood were on a collision course.

[4] I think motherhood is summed up best by a line from Karen Maezen

Miller's book *Momma Zen: Walking the Crooked Path of Motherhood*:

"The life of the mother is the life of the child: you are two blossoms on a single

branch." My son's smile brought back those words to me, and my joy was

<u>immeasurable.</u> 484
483

471. If the writer were to change the pronoun *us* to *me* in the preceding
sentence, this opening sentence would
(A) take on a less formal tone.
(B) indicate that the writer feels isolated.
(C) show that the topic is not personal.
(D) suggest that the writer has strong feelings.

472. (A) NO CHANGE
(B) Because
(C) Moreover,
(D) While

473. (A) NO CHANGE
(B) As an example,
(C) Considering
(D) OMIT the underlined portion.

474. (A) NO CHANGE
(B) found
(C) was finding
(D) was found

475. (A) NO CHANGE
(B) him. And to find
(C) him and find
(D) him, and find

476. (A) NO CHANGE
     (B) filled
     (C) were filled
     (D) was filling

477. (A) NO CHANGE
     (B) While taking
     (C) After he took
     (D) As he was taking

478. The writer is considering revising the preceding part of the sentence ("as if we hadn't met in ages") to read as follows:

> as if we hadn't seen each other in a long time

If the writer did this, the passage would primarily lose

(A) nothing of significance, since they mean the same thing.
(B) a detail that adds depth, as the expression "ages" connotes an extremely long time.
(C) a point that helps set the time and place of the passage.
(D) an indication that the mother feels old around her son.

479. The best placement for the underlined portion would be

(A) where it is now.
(B) at the beginning of the sentence, with a capital *W.*
(C) after the word *embarrassed.*
(D) after the word *mother.*

480. (A) NO CHANGE
     (B) laxity
     (C) confluence
     (D) loquaciousness

481. (A) NO CHANGE
     (B) had been having
     (C) had been
     (D) having

482. (A) NO CHANGE
     (B) pressure: plus
     (C) pressure plus
     (D) pressure, plus

483. Which of the alternatives to the underlined portion would NOT be acceptable?

(A) infinitesimal
(B) impressive
(C) boundless
(D) never-ending

484. For the sake of the logic and coherence of the essay, Paragraph 2 should be placed

(A) where it is now.
(B) at the beginning of the passage.
(C) after Paragraph 3.
(D) after Paragraph 4.

485. Suppose that the writer had intended to write a brief essay showing why the simplest and littlest things in life can surprise anybody and change the course of things. Would this essay satisfy that goal?

(A) Yes, because the essay shows that the writer finally learned how to be a good parent.
(B) Yes, because the essay shows that her son's smiling at her in school was so unexpected but, at the same time, so joyful, that her stress dissolved.
(C) No, because the focus of the essay is on how hard it is to be a mother these days.
(D) No, because the essay is not about her, but about how motherhood is different now than it was in simpler times.

The American Cowboy

Cowboys are an integral part of our history. While the first cowboys in
                                                       ‾‾‾‾
                                                        486
North America were the Mexican vaqueros. *Vaquero* means "cattle driver"

in Spanish. The vaqueros were very skilled on horseback and had been herding

cattle since the sixteenth century, when the conquistadors (soldiers of the Spanish

Empire) arrived from Spain 487 with horses and cattle. Many Anglos, or

English-speaking pioneers', moved into Texas beginning in 1821. They came
‾‾‾‾‾‾‾‾‾‾‾‾‾‾‾‾‾‾‾‾‾‾‾‾
         488
to round up the cattle that roam free on the plains. At that time, Texas was part
                            ‾‾‾‾‾‾‾‾‾
                              489

of Mexico. <u>Texas won its independence from Mexico in 1836; after the Battle of</u>
<u>San Jacinto,</u> when the Mexican general Santa Anna was defeated. <u>For instance,</u>
the Anglos took over the ranches that the Mexican owners <u>left behind them</u>
when they fled to Mexico. The Anglos hired the vaqueros to teach them the

cattle business. <u>These vaqueros trained Anglo cowboys.</u> They also gave the
English language new names for cowboys' equipment and activities. *Hacienda*

was the estate. *Rancho* was the ranch, and the *ranchero* worked on the ranch.

The leather pants called "chaps," which cowboys <u>wore protecting</u> their legs while
riding, got their name from the Spanish word *chaparajos*. So many Anglos

mispronounced the word *vaquero* <u>until it became</u> *buckaroo,* another name for
cowboy. The lariat that <u>cowboy used</u> to rope cattle got its name from the Spanish
la reata, which means "the long rope." *Rodeo* came from the Spanish word *rodear,*

which means "to round up cattle." The funny slang word for "jail": *hoosegow,*
was a garbled version of the Spanish word for "courtroom," *juzgado* (pronounced
/hooz-GAH-doh/).

When the end of the Civil War came, many flocked to the West for a new
life. The cowboy became a symbol of freedom, living on the open range, sleeping

under the stars. <u>Independently and self-reliantly,</u> the cowboy represented a
rugged individualism, a symbol of hard work and honor, freedom and strength.

There were cowgirls too, just as skilled as their male counterparts, handling cattle

on horseback.

In recognition of the cowboy's place in history, in 2005 the U.S. Senate

declared the fourth Saturday in July to be National Day of the American

Cowboy.

[1] In the twentieth century, this fascination with the life of the cowboy was reflected in hundreds of movies, with classic films like *3:10 to Yuma, Rio Grande,* and *High Noon.* [2] Even to this day, boys and girls dream of growing up to become a cowboy or a cowgirl. [3] Cowboys had their impact on TV also; shows like *Bonanza, The Lone Ranger,* and *Annie Oakley* were favorites. 500

486. (A) NO CHANGE
(B) Besides
(C) Indeed
(D) OMIT the underlined portion.

487. The writer is considering revising the preceding part of the sentence ("conquistadors (soldiers of the Spanish Empire) arrived from Spain") to read as follows:

   Spanish soldiers arrived from Spain

If the writer did this, the essay would primarily lose
(A) an historical detail that adds texture to the essay.
(B) a possible point of confusion over the word *conquistadors.*
(C) an indication that the Spanish Empire was far-reaching.
(D) nothing.

488. (A) NO CHANGE
(B) English-speaking pioneer's
(C) English-speaking pioneers
(D) English pioneers

489. (A) NO CHANGE
(B) roaming free
(C) roamed free
(D) roamed freely

490. (A) NO CHANGE
(B) Texas won its independence from Mexico in 1836. After the Battle of San Jacinto,
(C) Texas won its independence from Mexico in 1836, after the Battle of San Jacinto.
(D) Texas won its independence from Mexico in 1836, after the Battle of San Jacinto,

491. (A) NO CHANGE
  (B) Consequently,
  (C) As an example,
  (D) OMIT the underlined portion.

492. (A) NO CHANGE
  (B) leave behind them
  (C) left behind
  (D) leaving behind

493. (A) NO CHANGE
  (B) This vaquero trained Anglo cowboys.
  (C) Those vaqueros trained Anglo cowboys.
  (D) Whose vaqueros trained Anglo cowboys.

494. (A) NO CHANGE
  (B) wore protected
  (C) protected
  (D) wore to protect

495. (A) NO CHANGE
  (B) when it became
  (C) that it became
  (D) it became

496. (A) NO CHANGE
  (B) the cowboy use
  (C) the cowboy used
  (D) cowboys used

497. (A) NO CHANGE
  (B) "jail"—hoosegow—
  (C) "jail," hoosegow—
  (D) OMIT the underlined portion.

498. (A) NO CHANGE
  (B) When came the end of the Civil War,
  (C) With the end of the Civil War,
  (D) With the ending of the Civil War,

499. (A) NO CHANGE
    (B) Independent and self-reliant,
    (C) More independent and self-reliant,
    (D) Most independent and self-reliant,

500. Which of the following sequences of sentences makes the paragraph most logical?
    (A) NO CHANGE
    (B) 2, 1, 3
    (C) 1, 3, 2
    (D) 3, 2, 1

CHAPTER 7

How to Write an Essay

Writing can seem like a very intuitive process—either you get it or you don't. This leaves those who don't think they "get it" feeling hopeless. In part, this is because the writing process can be difficult to explain and can take practice before mastery is achieved.

The truth, however, is that there are steps that people can take to improve their writing skills. Specifically, when writing the ACT essay, there are strategies that can improve your grade. We will take you step-by-step through the process so that you clearly understand what to do. After you understand the steps to writing a good essay, the next part will be up to you: practice, practice, practice! Practicing writing an essay with a time constraint will help you be able to organize your time when you are taking the actual test.

Now, on to writing strategies!

The ACT gives you 40 minutes to write your essay. You need to give yourself a certain amount of time for each step of the process and remain aware of the clock so that you don't run out of time and have an unfinished essay.

You also want to clearly understand the instructions before you begin your essay. Luckily, although the writing prompts are always different, the instructions for the ACT essay remain that same. Therefore, you can be prepared before you ever walk in to take your test. ACT administrators want you to write an essay that is both persuasive and analytical. You must make sure to decide what your perspective on the argument is, and clearly argue for it. You will be graded on four points:

- Your ability to clearly state your perspective and analyze the relationship between your perspective and at least one other perspective that was given.
- Your ability to develop and support your ideas with reasoning and examples.
- Your ability to organize your ideas clearly and logically.
- Your ability to communicate your ideas effectively in standard written English.

These might seem like complicated instructions, but as we break them down, you will find they aren't as difficult as they seem.

When you take the test, you will be given a writing prompt and three perspectives. In this lesson, we will use a sample prompt so that you can watch the process unfold. This will be our sample:

The Electoral College in the United States

The Electoral College was established during the formation of our nation. It was adopted as a compromise by the framers of the Constitution. The smaller states did not want to pick the president by popular vote because they knew that in that type of election only the more populous states would have a say. An Electoral College gave the smaller states more of a voice, although they still did not have the influence that the larger states had. The Electoral College system also required 270 electoral votes to declare a winner. This virtually ensured that the federal government remained a two-party system.

A lot has changed over the 250 years since the Constitution was written. In the 2016 election, Hillary Clinton won the popular vote by receiving nearly 2.9 million more votes than Donald Trump. However, Donald Trump was awarded a decisive victory according to the electoral vote. This was the second time in recent history that the winner of the presidential race did not win the popular vote.

After the 2016 election, many people questioned the validity of having an Electoral College and wanted to abolish it. Others felt that the Electoral College was still an important tool. The restructuring of the electoral process in the United States would be a major change, but it is worth considering.

Perspective One

The Electoral College is an antiquated system that simply doesn't meet the modern needs of the United States. Each person's vote should be considered equal, and that only happens if the Electoral College is abolished. The popular vote is the best way to decide the presidency.

Perspective Two

The Electoral College is a brilliant innovation. It preserves the distribution of power between the states and federal government and allows the needs of all regions of the country to be considered at election time.

Perspective Three

The Electoral College system unfairly stifles third parties. This two-party system is crippling the government, and the Electoral College should be modernized to allow for more voices to be heard.

Organizing and Planning

You should allot yourself 8 to 10 minutes for this part. You might be tempted to just jump into writing to save time, but don't do it. Your essay will be much clearer if you organize and plan before you start writing. It will probably save you time in the long run also.

Step 1: Clearly Defining Perspectives

The first part of organizing your essay is making sure you understand the writing prompt and the three perspectives. Take time to read them carefully. Then, make a little note to sum up the position of each perspective. From the above sample, you could say:

- Perspective one: Get rid of Electoral College; elect by popular vote.
- Perspective two: Keep the Electoral College.
- Perspective three: Change the system to allow a third-party candidate.

You are allowed to either pick one of the perspectives given or come up with one of your own. You do not get extra points for coming up with your own perspective, and it will probably take up extra time, so your best bet is just to pick the perspective you think will be easiest to support with reasoning and examples.

Step 2: Listing Reasons and Examples

In this initial stage of organizing and planning, you don't have to be sure which perspective you will take, but you will probably have an idea. Use the back of the test or some scrap paper for your notes. Jot down some reasons and examples that would support each of the perspectives. The ACT only asks you to analyze the relationship between your perspective and one of the other ones given. Therefore, as long as you have reasons and examples for at least two of the perspectives, you are fine. If you can't think of any for the third perspective, don't worry about it.

When you are gathering reasons and examples, you can pull from a variety of sources. These include:

- Personal experience
- Historical or current events
- Statistics

The nice thing about this part is that the information can come from any of these sources. The ACT administrators don't care. As long as your essay is well organized and supported, you can use examples from any relevant historical event and get full points. Here are some examples that you might use for the sample essay:

- Perspective one: Get rid of Electoral College; elect by popular vote.
  - To be a true democracy, everyone's vote should have equal weight.
  - Votes don't have equal weight with the Electoral College because less populous states have more influence than they should.
- Perspective two: Keep the Electoral College
  - The Electoral College prevents third-party fringe ideas from gaining credibility, which allows for a more cohesive government.
  - When there are more than two parties it is hard to get anything done.
  - The Electoral College forces the candidates to address the concerns of all the states, not just the more populous urban centers.
  - The Electoral College gives power to the state instead of the federal government.
- Perspective three: Change the system to allow a third-party candidate.
  - This could add diversity to our government and allow more minority views to be heard.

Step 3: Brainstorming for Arguments Against Opposing Perspectives

As you made your list of reasons and examples, it probably became clearer to you which perspective you want to pick. That is great. This is the time to make a choice and stick to it. With our example prompt, let's choose perspective two. This allows us to argue against both perspective one and perspective three.

With any of these prompts, you can make a list of assumptions and consequences for each perspective you will argue against.

- Assumptions:
  - The popular vote is the best way to choose a president (perspective one).
  - The two-party system cripples the government (perspective three).

- Consequences:
  - The popular vote might be a good way to choose a president, but it could lead to the needs of whole regions of the country being ignored.
  - The two-party system has some drawbacks, but in governments that have more than two parties, getting a majority vote is very difficult. That can lead to no progress as legislation can be stalled indefinitely.

Step 4: Organizing Your Essay

This is a very important step. The ACT administrators will be looking carefully at how well you organize your essay. The most necessary part of a well-organized essay is a good thesis statement. A good thesis statement will present the topic and express your position in relation to the topic. It will let your readers know what you intend to prove in the essay.

Basically, you need to start with an introductory paragraph that contains your thesis statement. Then, you write body paragraphs. Start with the perspectives you are arguing against, examples, and counterarguments for them. Next, introduce the perspective you support and the reasons and examples you have. Finally, finish with a conclusion that sums up your argument.

In this step, all we do is formulate a thesis statement and organize the information that we already have. Because you are being timed, you could simply number the ideas that you have instead of rewriting them. (Put a #1 beside each idea that needs to go in body paragraph one, a #2 beside each idea for body paragraph two, and so forth.)

Here is a way to organize our sample essay:

The Electoral College

Thesis Statement

- The Electoral College is the best way for the United States to run its elections. (This is a rough version and needs to be fixed when the essay is written.)

Body Paragraph One

- Perspective one: get rid of Electoral College; elect by popular vote.
- To be a true democracy, everyone's vote should have equal weight.
- Votes don't have equal weight with the Electoral College because less populous states have more influence than they should.
- The popular vote is the best way to choose a president (perspective one).
- The popular vote might be a good way to choose a president, but it could lead to the needs of whole regions of the country being ignored.

Body Paragraph Two

- Perspective three: Change the system to allow a third-party candidate.
- This could add diversity to our government and allow more minority views to be heard.
- It could also hamper progress by creating a stalemate in the legislative process.
- The two-party system cripples the government (perspective three).
- The two-party system has some drawbacks, but in governments that have more than two parties, getting a majority vote is very difficult. That can lead to no progress as legislation can be stalled indefinitely.

Body Paragraph Three

- Perspective two: Keep the Electoral College.
- The Electoral College gives the states more power.
- It forces the candidates to address the concerns of all the states, not just the more populous urban centers.
- The Electoral College prevents third-party fringe ideas from gaining credibility, which allows for a more cohesive government. When there are more than two parties, it is hard to get anything done.

Conclusion

This is the last step in the planning and organizing stage of our essay writing. Make sure to keep an eye on the clock during this time and try not to spend more than 10 minutes total on this. If you do, you will have to skimp on the actual writing. In general, your conclusion should restate the main point of your essay.

Writing Your Essay

You should have about 30 minutes left, but you want to save a little time for revising and proofreading, so try to get the writing done in about 25 minutes.

Step 5: Introductory Paragraph and Thesis Statement

Think of your introductory paragraph as a funnel. Start the paragraph with a large idea that will grab everyone's attention. Narrow that thought down in the next few sentences and end with your thesis statement, which should be a concise sentence about the focus of this essay. You can incorporate ideas from the writing prompt in the introductory paragraph. (If you are unable to come up with an introductory paragraph quickly, you can skip it and come back to it later—but remember to leave room!)

Consider this sample introductory paragraph:

> *The United States is known as the Land of the Free, and we are proud of the many cherished liberties that are offered to our citizens. Perhaps the most valued of those rights is the right to elect our leaders. Every four years, most adults have the opportunity to vote for the person they think is deserving of the office of the Presidency of the United States. Lately, however, much controversy has arisen because the winner of the popular vote has not been the person elected to that office. Instead, the president was the winner of the Electoral College vote.*

Your final sentence should be your thesis statement. It should clearly state your perspective and show how it contrasts with at least one other idea from the prompt. Here is a thesis statement for our sample:

Although many people consider the Electoral College undemocratic, it is actually a brilliant system created by the Constitution that allows all citizens in the nation to feel represented in the presidential election process.

In this sample, the introductory paragraph has created a "funnel." It starts with a wide idea to capture everyone's attention (the United States has many liberties) and narrows it down until it is focused on the specific subject of the essay (the Electoral College is a brilliant system).

Step 6: Body Paragraphs

Body paragraph one should discuss one of the perspectives you are arguing against. First, explain the perspective, and then list the reasons and examples that support it. Finally, counter these reasons using the assumptions and consequences that you have listed.

Our sample prompt could have a first body paragraph like this:

One common argument against the Electoral College (as seen in perspective one) is that it is undemocratic. The electoral votes are based on population, with larger states receiving a greater number of votes. However, less populous states have more electoral votes than they would if the vote were based strictly on population. This means "one person, one vote" is not necessarily true. Many people consider this very undemocratic. Although this is a valid argument, this perspective does not consider the whole picture. States were awarded electoral votes to ensure that they were represented despite their populations. This important fact allows all regions of our country to feel represented in the election.

You do not have to discuss both of the perspectives that you did not choose. However, if you have time and ideas, you can make body paragraph two about the second perspective that you are disagreeing with. Use the same format that you used in body paragraph one, but make sure you use transitions from one paragraph to the next. The transition can be as simple as "In contrast to perspective one," or "Similar to perspective one."

Our sample essay could have a second body paragraph like this:

Similar to perspective one, perspective three argues that the Electoral College is antiquated and needs to be abolished or at least revised. Its main argument is that the need for a clear majority of electoral votes forces the United States to remain a two-party system. Thus, third-party candidates cannot win and fringe candidates are unable to gain traction for their ideas. This is true, but I would argue that it is not a bad thing. A multi-party system can completely stall the legislative process because there is no clear majority. Take France, for instance. France is often unable to get any major new legislation passed for years because its legislative branch is made up of politicians from many different parties that can't work together to agree on anything. Political stalemate is one of the very real dangers of multi-party systems, and the Electoral College was created to guard against that very thing.

For the next body paragraphs, you should introduce the perspective that you are arguing for. Give your reason for supporting this perspective, and then use your examples or facts to support your position. Try to connect your examples to your thesis statement. This might become a couple of paragraphs as you elaborate on your argument. Make sure to also link your argument back to the counterarguments that you have already made about the other perspectives.

The final body paragraphs of our essay could be something like this:

> *I agree with perspective one that it is very important to safeguard our democratic elections. This is a core element of what makes the United States a free country. I think, however, that we need to carefully consider the benefits of the Electoral College instead of just embracing the idea of election by popular vote. The Constitution is carefully structured to balance the powers of the state and federal governments. The Electoral College gives power to the state. This is another way that the states are able to have their issues represented in the federal government.*
>
> *The country is already starkly divided between red and blue states. In the 2016 campaign, Clinton and Trump spent a majority of their time, resources, and money trying to win just a few states. The rest of the states were already decided. Imagine a system that allowed election of the president by popular vote. The majority of the population of the United States is in New York and California. Presidential candidates would not have to address issues that affect rural America at all. In fact, because urban issues and rural issues are often at odds, presidential candidates would most likely champion urban causes to the detriment of rural citizens. This would lead to many citizens feeling alienated and frustrated.*

Finally, create a conclusion. This can be as simple as one statement. If you have time, you can relate a few examples back to the thesis or add some sentences that sum up your main idea. Be sure to end by restating your thesis in a way that wraps up your essay.

Our conclusion could be something like this:

> *I fully agree that it is important to address the concerns of all the citizens in our nation. It is also important to consider carefully the ramifications of our election system to make sure it suits our needs. However, when the Electoral College is put under careful scrutiny, I think that we find it does exactly what it was created to do. It safeguards our governmental structure, it gives power to the states, and it allows citizens to feel like they are involved in the election process. In short, it is still an important and relevant part of the election process in the United States.*

Step 7: Revising and Proofreading

Hopefully you have a few minutes left after you have written your essay. If you do, use it to read over your essay and correct any mistakes. Look for mistakes in grammar and punctuation, of course, but also be on the lookout for repetitive phrasing and any sentences that are unclear.

Here is a final look at our sample essay:

> *The United States is known as the Land of the Free, and we are proud of the many cherished liberties that are offered to our citizens. Perhaps the most valued of those rights is the right to elect our leaders. Every four years, most adults have the opportunity to vote for the person they think is deserving of the office of the Presidency of the United States. Lately, however, much controversy has arisen because the winner of the popular vote has not been the person elected to that office. Instead, the president was the winner of the Electoral College vote. Although many people consider the Electoral College undemocratic, it is actually a brilliant system created by the Constitution that allows all citizens in the nation to feel represented in the presidential election process.*
>
> *One common argument against the Electoral College (as seen in perspective one) is that it is undemocratic. The electoral votes are based on population, with larger states receiving a greater number of votes. However, less populous states have more electoral votes than they would if the vote were based strictly on population. This means "one person, one vote" is not necessarily true. Many people consider this very undemocratic. Although this is a valid argument, this perspective does not consider the whole picture. States were awarded electoral votes to ensure that they were represented despite their populations. This important fact allows all regions of our country to feel represented in the election.*
>
> *Similar to perspective one, perspective three argues that the Electoral College is antiquated and needs to be abolished or at least revised. Its main argument is that the need for a clear majority of electoral votes forces the United States to remain a two-party system. Thus, third-party candidates cannot win and fringe candidates are unable to gain traction for their ideas. This is true, but I would argue that it is not a bad thing. A multi-party system can completely stall the legislative process because there is no clear majority. Take France, for instance. France is often unable to get any major new legislation passed for years because its legislative branch is made up of politicians from many different parties that can't work together to agree on anything. Political stalemate is one of the very real dangers of multi-party systems, and the Electoral College was created to guard against that very thing.*
>
> *I agree with perspective one that it is very important to safeguard our democratic elections. This is a core element of what makes the United States a free country. I think, however, that we need to carefully consider*

the benefits of the Electoral College instead of just embracing the idea of election by popular vote. The Constitution is carefully structured to balance the powers of the state and federal governments. The Electoral College gives power to the state. This is another way that the states are able to have their issues represented in the federal government.

The country is already starkly divided between red and blue states. In the 2016 campaign, Clinton and Trump spent a majority of their time, resources, and money trying to win just a few states. The rest of the states were already decided. Imagine a system that allowed election of the president by popular vote. The majority of the population of the United States is in New York and California. Presidential candidates would not have to address issues that affect rural America at all. In fact, because urban issues and rural issues are often at odds, presidential candidates would most likely champion urban causes to the detriment of rural citizens. This would lead to many citizens feeling alienated and frustrated.

I fully agree that it is important to address the concerns of all the citizens in our nation. It is also important to consider carefully the ramifications of our election system to make sure it suits our needs. However, when the Electoral College is put under careful scrutiny, I think that we find it does exactly what it was created to do. It safeguards our governmental structure, it gives power to the states, and it allows citizens to feel like they are involved in the election process. In short, it is still an important and relevant part of the election process in the United States.

As you read over your essay, you might notice a few mistakes. Just cross out neatly and insert your correction.

There. You are finished!

Learning to write well can be time consuming, but it is worth it. The best thing you can do to boost your ACT Writing score is follow these steps and continue to practice. You will get better with every try!

CHAPTER 8

ACT Essay Prompts

Prompt 1

Historical Revisionism

Historical revisionism is the reevaluation of historical events and figures with the introduction of new facts that change the way these events and figures are viewed. Sometimes, instead of new facts, a new moral compass is used. People who were once viewed as heroes become villains, and those once viewed as villains may become heroes. Some view this restatement of historical data as positive, while others view it negatively. It is certainly worth debating.

Perspective One

Simply because someone or some event has always been viewed in a positive light is no reason that we should refuse to dig deeper. If we blindly accept the attitudes taught to us by our forebears, we cannot grow and learn from our history. As we evolve, we need to reevaluate history as we know it.

Perspective Two

It is wrong to impose a modern morality on the people and events that took place in history. Through that lens, there would be no heroes. Instead, we must look at them through the context of the time in which they lived or took place. That is the only way to clearly judge a person or situation.

Perspective Three

No person is without flaws; no event is without some negative repercussions. If we dig long and hard enough, we will find something to despise about every hero. Removing the heroes from our culture will have negative consequences. Instead of searching for flaws, we should celebrate the great achievements without trying to tear our historical icons apart.

Prompt 2

Vegans Versus Meat-Eaters

The debate between vegans and meat-eaters wages on. The question of whether or not people should eat meat has been sparking heated debates for many years. While many people feel that it is healthier to eschew meats, others are just as ardent in their espousal of incorporating meat into their daily diets. Some people go vegan for health reasons, while others feel morally bound to avoid eating other animals. This issue affects everyone on a daily basis and should be examined carefully.

Perspective One

Our ancestors have thrived on meat for millennia. Our bodies, just like theirs, are biologically programmed to consume meat. The truth is we eat meat, we love meat, and we are built to digest meat. There should be no shame in consuming meat as part of our diets. We are simply doing what our bodies were designed to do, and we are healthier for it.

Perspective Two

Contrary to the reports of many meat-eaters, studies have shown that vegetarians live longer, healthier lives. Partly this is because meat is hard on the digestive system. We can get all the nutrients we need from a plant-based diet and will be healthier for it.

Perspective Three

Whether or not eating meat is good for our bodies, it is a selfish food choice. It is not just a nutritional issue, it is a moral one. We should not be depriving other animals of life simply because they taste good to us. In addition to causing murder, a meat-eating society is harmful to the environment as many resources go into raising livestock.

Prompt 3

Should Children Work?

Society has come a long way since the days when children as young as six or seven worked twelve-hour days for about $1 a week. Since then, laws have been enacted to protect children from the ruthless exploitation of the early industrialization period. While no one argues that we should return to those practices, some people think that as a society we overprotect our children from work. Perhaps instead of being helped, young people are being hurt by a society that doesn't think children should be made to work. How young is too young?

At what age is it okay to require labor from children? This debate involves parents, social workers, and business owners.

Perspective One

In the United States today, people have been so concerned about making sure that children are not overworked that we have created another problem. We have whole generations of children growing up without learning about responsibility or work ethic. Children should be encouraged to work at a young age so that they can become responsible adults.

Perspective Two

Although some responsibility at home is good for children, they should not be allowed into the workplace until they are fourteen. This will prevent businesses from exploiting them as a cheap labor pool. Child labor is a slippery slope, and stringent laws are needed to keep history from repeating itself.

Perspective Three

Children should not have to work when they are young. Youth is a time for freedom and for learning new things. There is plenty of time for responsibility and working when they become adults. As a society, we owe it to children to give them a carefree youth.

ANSWERS

Chapter 1: Set 1 Reading Questions

1. (B) The narrator isn't a scientist, so answer choice (A) is incorrect. There is no mention of a friend of the man, so answer choice (C) is incorrect. The narrator is clearly not the man himself, so answer choice (D) is incorrect.

2. (D) This is a metaphor and uses words that would typically describe a candle.

3. (C) The language that is used to describe the man sounds more like a description of some beast. The other answer choices aren't suggested by the passage.

4. (C) There is enough food onboard, so answer choice (A) is incorrect. The scientists treated the man with respect, so answer choice (B) is incorrect. The ship is going to San Francisco, but that isn't the man's concern, so answer choice (D) is incorrect.

5. (B) This is what the simile suggests, that to the man the food was like gold.

6. (A) The man feared that he would run out of food.

7. (A) A *mendicant* is a beggar—someone who has nothing and asks for money or food.

8. (C) They were eating food that he thought he would need when there was another famine.

9. (B) The sailors smiled and gave him their biscuits; they thought he was a curiosity. There is no indication that the sailors were afraid of the man, so answer choice (A) is incorrect. Neither answer choice (C) nor answer choice (D) is supported by the passage.

10. (B) Although it is suggested that he told the scientists his name, it isn't revealed in the passage.

11. (B) This is what the experiences of the man suggest. The other answer choices aren't consistent with the passage.

12. (A) This is what the scientists thought would happen and what did happen.

13. (B) The fact that the man nearly starved to death has impacted the way he thinks and acts. The other answer choices refer to aspects of the story, but they aren't the main theme.

14. (B) This is the main reason the passage was written and what the author wanted to achieve.

15. (D) A close reading of the passage makes this the clear answer choice. While (C) is probably true, the passage notes that the stilts were helpful in navigating undrained marshes.

16. (A) This shows how well the race was greeted by the people of the area. The other answer choices don't reflect their enthusiasm.

17. (A) While the route was chosen by the organizers of the race, they did not choose it because of the number of cafés. Familiarity with the route is not discussed in the passage, making answer choice (C) unlikely, and the passage also does not state whether the route went through well-populated areas, making answer choice (D) incorrect.

18. (C) The word *narrowed* means "became fewer" in this case.

19. (C) Although a newspaper did increase its readership by sponsoring this event, this is not the main point of the passage because that idea is not discussed in depth. In addition, it only addresses one particular newspaper's tactics, so (A) is not correct. Maurice Garin is mentioned, but he is not the focal point of the passage, so (B) is not correct. A slight mention of the difference between the first Tour de France and the modern one is made, but that is quickly passed by, so (D) is not correct. The answer is (C) because the last two paragraphs of the passage are devoted to describing the many problems with cheating.

20. (D) *Unscrupulous* means to not be honest or fair or having or showing no moral principle.

21. (A) The idea that cyclists could ride for 17 hours at almost exactly the same average speed is surprising. There is no suggestion in the passage that any of the other reasons were surprising.

22. (B) The last sentence of the first paragraph states that the racers were "spurred on" by the "enticement" of the reward. This language suggests that the reward was significant. The passage doesn't mention fame or the feelings of the competitors toward one another, so none of the other choices are correct.

23. (D) The passage states that the stages were so long that "the cyclists rode through the night." From this you can infer that they had to endure a lack of sleep. The passage does mention that Garin was accused of illegally obtaining food (B), but it doesn't go into enough detail to determine that all the racers lacked sufficient food.

24. (A) Passage 1 never mentions that there was any cheating or other moral issues with the competitors or the fans. Passage 2, on the other hand, goes into detail about the underhanded tactics that were used. The issues of who should participate (B) and having too much publicity (C) are not really addressed in the passages. Although there is a large reward given in Passage 2 (D), there is also a reward in Passage 1, so a clear difference is not made.

25. (C) Both passages enumerate the difficulties of the endurance races they describe. Although the author of Passage 2 would agree that there are many ways to cheat (A), there was no mention of this in Passage 1. There is no comparison of modern races in Passage 1 (B), and there is no mention of a final celebration in Passage 2 (D).

26. (B) In both passages, the idea for the race was conceived as a way to boost newspaper sales. Although the races probably also accomplished all the other choices also, that was not their impetus (motivation).

27. (A) Passage 1 indicates that fan participation was a good thing as people watched, handed racers drinks, and celebrated the victory. Passage 2 shows the negative side of fan participation as it describes fans sabotaging other competitors and beating them up.

28. (C) Specifically, Washington notes that "there were at least a half-dozen other places in the cabin that would have accommodated the cats" (lines 12–13). Based on this information, as well as on an earlier description of the room as having "openings in the side" (line 3), answer choice (C) is most supported by information in the passage.

29. (C) This is the best answer choice. Since Washington is telling about his childhood in detail, answer choices (A) and (D) are unlikely. Washington addresses his family's desperate situation, so answer choice (B) is incorrect.

30. (B) The family did not have enough food, and the mother was trying to feed them.

31. (C) Eating the roasted sweet potatoes was a joy to Washington.

32. (A) This is the intent of the paragraph. There is no comparison, so answer choice (B) is incorrect. Washington isn't complaining, so answer choice (C) is incorrect. He isn't being careful about how he talks about the conditions—he is blunt—so answer choice (D) is incorrect.

33. (A) He thought it was similar to being in paradise, not an easy option for a young slave. Answer choice (B) doesn't relate to the passage. Washington doesn't seem fearful of trying school, so answer choice (C) is incorrect. The passage doesn't mention answer choice (D).

34. (D) This is the one memory that Washington doesn't reveal.

35. (A) This was surprising to Washington; the other answer choices were not.

36. (D) This was the means by which the slaves acquired information.

37. (B) This is the author's intent. While the Civil War is mentioned, it isn't the main point of the passage, so answer choice (A) is incorrect.

38. (B) This seems to be the attitude the author has as he talks about his youth; there is no sense of anger or fear, so answer choices (A) and (C) are incorrect. Certainly, the author doesn't have an attitude of indifference or boredom about the hardships he endured in the past, so answer choice (D) is incorrect.

39. (A) Washington states that he "went as far as the schoolhouse door with one of my young mistresses" (line 41). The daughter of the plantation owner would be referred to by a slave as "my young mistress," making answer choice (A) the most plausible.

40. (B) The passage says that this was the first time that Washington realized he was a slave and, therefore, not free.

41. (C) A *contrivance* is a device or gadget.

42. (D) Answer choices (A), (B), and (C) are all contradicted in the passage.

43. (A) A close reading of the passage makes this the clear answer choice. The subjects in the other answer choices may have been written down, but the passage says that keeping track of personal possessions was a likely impetus for the development of writing.

44. (C) This was the advantage of picture symbols.

45. (B) Scribes helped rulers keep track of the collection of taxes, but the scribes were not rulers themselves, so answer choice (B) is more accurate than answer choice (A). Answer choice (C) covers a later topic, alphabets. Answer choice (D) may be true, but it is not supported by the passage.

46. (D) Although this isn't directly stated in the passage, this conclusion is probable. Writing a symbol instead of drawing a jar would be a much faster way to keep track of what has been paid.

47. (A) Both the United States and Sweden use the same signs for numbers; this can be inferred from the information in the passage.

48. (B) It is theorized that merchants in the Middle East (in modern Lebanon, Israel, and Syria) made the first alphabet. Answer choice (D) is tempting, since both of these ancient countries had alphabets, but they were not the first.

49. (B) Picture writing and hieroglyphics both preceded an alphabet. No alphabet was created before any language was spoken, so answer choice (C) is incorrect.

50. (A) Logically, it would have to be English; all of the other languages predate English.

51. (A) According to the passage, this is the reason that English is difficult to spell.

52. (D) The passage clearly states that written Chinese is composed of picture symbols.

53. (C) Certainly, the author doesn't believe that knowing how to write creates problems, so answer choice (A) is incorrect, nor would the author agree with answer choice (B) or answer choice (D).

54. (A) This is the main reason that an alphabet is superior to a system of symbols. More people can learn it more easily, which means more people can learn to read and write.

55. (C) This is the meaning of the word *immaterial.*

56. (B) The reader is told about O. Henry's background being in federal prison, so this is an easy inference to make.

57. (A) This is a figurative use of *bracelet.* There is no mention of a present, so answer choice (B) is incorrect. There is no mention that the bracelet was worth a lot of money, so answer choice (C) is incorrect.

58. (D) Soon after Easton bemoans his lack of money and high social standing, he implies that the ambassador does not have these problems. Miss Fairchild interrupts him to state that the ambassador "doesn't call any more." The exchange makes it plausible that both men were vying for Miss Fairchild's attention and that Easton was jealous of the ambassador's money and social prominence.

59. (B) The reader can determine this from the clues that the author gives about how Miss Fairchild feels about Easton, such as in the tenth paragraph, when the author says that she answers Easton "warmly."

60. (B) The fact that he was handcuffed and a prisoner of the marshal was embarrassing to him.

61. (B) Easton tells Miss Fairchild that the days of having fun are over for him; he is serious now. This is the figurative meaning of "butterfly days."

62. (B) The marshal feels that if the conversation continues, Miss Fairfield will realize that Easton is the prisoner, not the marshal.

63. (A) He notices the handcuff is on Easton's right hand.

64. (D) This is the figurative meaning of money "taking wings," that is, flying away.

65. (C) The passage says that the "look in the girl's eyes slowly changed to a bewildered horror" (lines 22–23).

66. (A) The man is following the conversation and then reacts to it. It is unlikely he was trying to impress Miss Fairchild, so answer choice (B) is incorrect. He probably doesn't know why Easton came to the West, so answer choice (C) is incorrect.

67. (B) This surprise ending is typical of O. Henry.

68. (A) We can see through his actions that he is trying to help Easton in a difficult situation.

69. (B) The paragraphs don't mention why she is on the train.

Chapter 2: Set 2 Reading Questions

70. (B) This is the point of view from which the story is told. There is no evidence that the narrator rode on the fox hunt, is a member of the Paddock family, or has no riding ability.

71. (B) The sentence "Travers had never ridden; but he had been prompted how to answer by Miss Paddock" (lines 14–15) makes answer choice (B) the best response.

72. (C) This doesn't pose a reason to fear riding Monster; the other answer choices do.

73. (B) Travers was worried about what he was told about the horse. There is no evidence that he was anxious about getting married, had a fever, or had indigestion.

74. (D) Before the ride, Travers is worried about his riding skills, since he knows he will be judged by his fiancée's family in that regard. Once Travers learns that he will be riding a horse that has killed a man, his fear grows even worse.

75. (A) For much of the ride, as Monster races ahead of the other horses, Travers has his eyes closed and is more or less clinging to the horse for dear life. Answer choice (A) best conveys this state of affairs.

76. (B) The passage indicates that Travers tried to get Monster to the bridge, but the horse would not comply.

77. (B) A locomotive "jumping the ties" is out of control and cannot be controlled.

78. (D) Although the passage doesn't explicitly state young Paddock's motivation, this reason must be closest to the truth. Clearly, Monster was not the best horse, so answer choice (A) is incorrect. The passage doesn't mention a desire to upset his sister, so answer choice (B) is incorrect. It is doubtful that, considering what young Paddock said about Monster, he was trying to please Travers, so answer choice (C) is incorrect.

79. (A) This is what the simile means.

80. (A) The sacrifice was what he endured to gain the respect of his fiancée's family. The other answer choices would not have been sacrifices.

81. (B) This is what *nonchalant* means.

82. (A) The story is extremely amusing, but highly improbable.

83. (D) This is the correct description of Travers. He was willing to do anything to please his bride-to-be and gain the admiration of her family.

84. (D) The other answer choices are mentioned in the speech, but they aren't the main point of the second paragraph.

85. (B) This is the meaning of the metaphor.

86. (A) King wants to dramatize the situation.

87. (D) This sentence speaks of transforming our nation into a symphony of brotherhood; it is hopeful. The other sentences don't support the idea that King has hope for a better world.

88. (C) Manacles and chains evoke the image of a jail. A person would not be chained in a hospital or at work, and chains would not keep him safe.

89. (C) This is what King is suggesting. The other answer choices aren't supported by the passage.

90. (A) He repeats three times, "Now is the time . . .". He doesn't use the word *slowly*, so answer choice (B) is incorrect. He doesn't advocate preserving segregation, so answer choice (C) is incorrect. There is no mention in the speech of holding a vote on civil rights, so answer choice (D) is incorrect.

91. (D) King is saying that the suffering endured by African-Americans at the hands of the police can be called godly. There is no mention of suffering being productive, so answer choice (A) is incorrect. King doesn't use the word *evil*, so answer choice (B) is incorrect. While it could be inferred that those who have suffered have faith (answer choice (C)), answer choice (D) is more accurate.

92. (C) Here, the verb *wallow* means "to roll about lazily." *Self-indulgent* is a close synonym.

93. (A) There is no indication that going back to the slums and ghettos in the North would be a hardship. The hardships are police brutality, racial injustice, and the fact that, 100 years after the Emancipation Proclamation, African-Americans are still not free.

94. (C) Just as Americans in colonial days dreamed of freedom from British rule, King dreams of freedom from oppression for his people. He doesn't mention that his dream is difficult to understand, so answer choice (A) is incorrect. He doesn't talk of an African-American dream, so answer choice (B) is incorrect. He exhorts the audience to return to wherever they are from, South or North, and work to make the dream of freedom a reality.

95. (D) King paints a grim portrait of the governor of Alabama. *Interposition* and *nullification* are strong words. Indeed, two months earlier, the governor had blocked the enrollment of African-American students at the University of Alabama. There is no sign of giving up hope in the paragraph, so answer choice (A) is incorrect. Certainly, the last thing the governor wants to see are white and black children playing together, so answer choice (B) is incorrect. Although the word *dripping* is suggestive, King is merely using a strong metaphor, so answer choice (C) is incorrect.

96. (A) The metaphorical "sculpture" is a huge task, but it does represent the beginning of hope for freedom for all African-Americans. Creation of an actual sculpture isn't discussed, so answer choice (B) is incorrect.

97. (B) King means that freedom will ring for all Americans; "God's children" refers to all human beings. King doesn't say that music is liberating, so answer choice (A) is incorrect. The song wouldn't have a new meaning, so answer choice (D) is incorrect.

98. (D) The author does like the doll, but that isn't the main point of the passage, so answer choice (A) is incorrect. The passage doesn't argue against funding for the disabled, so answer choice (B) is incorrect. The passage doesn't support laws that protect the disabled, so answer choice (C) is incorrect.

99. (B) When something is confounded, it is confused or mixed up. The other answer choices don't signify *confounding*.

100. (D) Those barriers were swept away, and Helen went on to have a remarkable career.

101. (B) A key piece of information is the sentence "I knew then that "w-a-t-e-r" meant the wonderful cool something that was flowing over my hand." This statement, and the text surrounding it, makes answer choice (B) correct.

102. (D) The experience created a sense of joy in Helen; it set her free. Communication was not impossible, as she found out, so answer choice (A) is incorrect; it certainly wasn't upsetting (answer choice (B)) or inevitable (answer choice (C)).

103. (A) Although the passage does show the way Howe dealt with a person with disabilities (B), that was a particular case and not the main point of the passage. Similarly, it does show us that Howe was a brilliant teacher, but that is not the focus of the passage. It mentions in passing that a dog could have done some of the same tricks, but that certainly isn't the focus of the passage. The whole passage leads up to the moment when Bridgman's mind is awakened and her intellect ignited (A).

104. (C) Here, the author compared what Bridgman was doing to what a dog could do. That was so that he could later contrast this to her behavior when she began using a higher intelligence.

105. (B) Bridgman was using spoons (D), but the passage doesn't actually imply that she enjoyed this. It does indicate that she liked to be patted on the head because "she was encouraged" by this. Although the paragraph does show that she is learning (C), it doesn't indicate that she was exceptional, nor does it indicate how she felt about her teacher (A).

106. (D) Although labeling did teach a blind person to read (A), the method was not compared to other methods. The personality of Howe (C) is not really addressed. It was not learning to read (B) but, rather, learning to communicate that sparked Bridgman's intellect.

107. (A) It is apparent from the discussion of his methods that Howe used structure and persistence to reach Bridgman. (B) and (C) couldn't be true or his methods wouldn't have worked. (D) could be true, but there is no evidence to support that.

108. (B) Passage 1 was an autobiography, so it showed the author's feelings, which gave it a personal tone. Passage 2 was related through the teacher's voice and sounded as though he were talking about an experiment he had conducted. It was much less personal than the first passage.

109. (B) Both of the passages describe blind and deaf children who realize for the first time that they can use words to communicate.

110. (C) Both of the passages make some use of similes or metaphors (A), relate a step-by-step process (B), and offer a description of techniques (D). Because Passage 1 is an autobiography, it also makes use of internal feelings to explain a transformation.

111. (C) Both of the passages end with the girls realizing that words express meaning and indicate that this will change their lives. Passage 2 does not relate the moment when Bridgman met her teacher (A). Although it was an important step for them to learn to spell (B), this did not release their intellect. Passage 2 does not contain any information about Bridgman going outside (D).

112. (C) These people are ambidextrous and can use either hand for any purpose.

113. (D) *Etiology* is the cause of a condition or a disease. *Custom* (answer choice (A)) and *essence* (answer choice (B)) don't make sense in the context of the paragraph. While *effect* (answer choice (C)) could possibly be correct, a close reading makes *cause* the best answer.

114. (B) This is clearly stated in the third paragraph. Nowhere does the article state that left-handed people are happier (answer choice (A)) or that too much effort is given to the topic (answer choice (C)). The passage does say that a large preponderance of successful sports figures are left-handed, but doesn't make the same claim for musicians, so answer choice (D) is incorrect.

115. (A) The fourth paragraph states that "lefties are often leaders in their fields." Answer choices (B) and (C) are touched on, but they aren't the main point of the passage; they are only examples that support the main point.

116. (D) The author uses Queen Elizabeth and her family as an example of how left-handedness runs in families. Answer choices (A), (B), and (C) may be true, but none of them is the reason for including the queen in the passage.

117. (C) Handedness isn't a significant factor in computer use.

118. (C) Dr. A. Klar argued in 2000 that right-handedness is determined by traits inherited from parents. Dr. Coren (answer choice (B)) thinks that preference for the left hand is due to mild brain injury, while Daniel Geschwind (answer choice (A)) believes that both of these, in addition to events early in life, are the cause. The passage states that Albert Einstein was left-handed, but he didn't focus on the study of left-handedness, so answer choice (D) is incorrect.

119. (B) The first paragraph states that 90 percent of people are right-handed.

120. (B) The passage states that scientists are "almost unanimous in arguing against" (lines 46–47) tying "the child's left hand behind its back" (lines 43–44).

121. (D) The passage states that most power tools are made for right-handed people. The passage states that there are cooking utensils for left-handed people, so answer choice (A) is incorrect. The passage states that there are books on how to play the guitar with the left hand, so answer choice (B) is incorrect. The passage states that lefties can use a computer if the mouse is switched to the left side, so answer choice (C) is incorrect.

122. (B) The passage doesn't mention legs, biting fingernails, or the size of one's hand.

123. (B) While answer choice (D) may be tempting, nothing in the passage indicates that left-handed people are more intelligent, although it strongly suggests that many lefties excel at what they do. The passage does say that left-handed scissors are available, so one can infer that lefties have trouble with ordinary scissors.

124. (A) Judging from the number of left-handed people and their need for products that are easier to use, this answer choice makes the most sense. Answer choice (B) may be true, but it is impossible to infer this from the seventh paragraph.

125. (B) The desk problem is pointed out in the passage. Seating left-handed students together in the classroom would be of no benefit, although it might benefit them in the cafeteria, so answer choice (A) is incorrect.

Chapter 3: Set 3 Reading Questions

126. (A) This is what Ivan fears if his wife wins the lottery. Answer choice (B) obviously doesn't pose a problem. Answer choices (C) and (D) are mentioned in the passage, but they aren't the main conflict.

127. (A) Ivan responded to the number as a baby would—a baby who did not really know what was going on, but reacted instinctually.

128. (B) The narrator certainly understands human nature and how it affects the situation.

129. (B) Ivan is contemplating how rainy and miserable autumn is.

130. (B) Masha doesn't want to give the money to her husband, so answer choice (A) is incorrect. Ivan doesn't want to buy his wife clothing, so answer choice (C) is incorrect. Nothing in the passage suggests that Masha would leave her husband, so answer choice (D) is incorrect.

131. (C) There is no indication that his wife no longer is in love with him, so answer choice (A) is incorrect. It is unlikely that his wife has worked harder than Ivan has, so answer choice (B) is incorrect. There is no evidence that Ivan is younger than his wife, so answer choice (D) is incorrect.

132. (B) This is what Ivan imagines will happen (lines 67–69).

133. (A) Both Ivan and Masha have daydreams of what it would be like to win the lottery.

134. (D) The word *begrudge* means "to resent," so it is clear that the author means that Ivan thought that Masha would be stingy.

135. (D) This is the reason Ivan did not immediately look to find out the winning number. Nothing in the passage suggests that the other answer choices are correct.

136. (A) Both Ivan and Masha fantasize about winning the lottery, and both go from being positive about each other to being angry with each other.

137. (D) After Ivan and Masha learn that they have not won the lottery, their notion about their lives has changed for the worse.

138. (D) Greed in this case pitted husband against wife.

139. (C) Cain uses the word *underscored* to emphasize the need.

140. (D) A close reading of the passage indicates that in the event that no candidate has received enough Electoral College votes, the House of Representatives decides who the next president will be.

141. (A) This is Cain's main point. The other answer choices are merely details.

142. (C) Electors aren't bound to vote for the choice of the people, which means they are free to vote for whomever they want. Answer choice (A) isn't relevant, and answer choice (B) isn't true. Answer choice (D) could happen but doesn't happen often.

143. (B) The candidate who wins the popular vote in a state gets all of the state's electoral votes, so in effect the vote is a vote for Candidate B.

144. (B) The word *anachronism* means something that is out-of-date or old-fashioned.

145. (C) The Constitution is updated by adopting amendments. The other answer choices are mentioned in the passage, but they don't support this statement.

146. (D) This isn't one of the reasons that the Electoral College system should be abandoned.

147. (B) The word *defecting* means "abandoning."

148. (B) She worries that American voters are losing faith in a system that they cannot directly affect.

149. (A) Cain would be most likely to support a thorough review, because she is suggesting that the Constitution be updated.

150. (D) The League of Women Voters wants to reinvigorate the voters in the country so they will be more interested in having their voices heard.

151. (D) Cain uses this example to demonstrate how little it would take to change the outcome of elections and bypass the choice of the people.

152. (A) This is the author's main point; she wants Congress to adopt an amendment that would abandon the Electoral College system.

153. (C) The women wanted to see if the sap was flowing so they could tap the trees. The sentence doesn't refer to making canoes, gathering wood, or making fires, so the other answer choices are incorrect.

154. (B) While the grandmother does seem lenient about the boys' tasting the syrup (answer choice (C)), this isn't her chief quality.

155. (C) The author was proud of his grandmother's industry. None of the other answer choices is suggested by the passage.

156. (D) The grandmother seemed to be the one who was running the maple sugar project. There is no evidence that she did not want to participate in the sugar gathering, so answer choice (A) is incorrect. There is no evidence that she thought her grandson was working too hard, so answer choice (B) is incorrect.

157. (A) The author thinks back on his childhood with warmth.

158. (B) This is expressed in the opening lines "Savages we call them, because their Manners differ from ours, which we think the Perfection of Civility. They think the same of theirs." Although options (A), (C), and (D) may be indicated by the passage, they are not the main point.

159. (C) This in expressed in the sentence: "for all their Government is by Counsel of the Sages." The next line, "there is no Force, there are no Prisons, no Officers to compel Obedience, or inflict Punishment," contradicts any of the other choices.

160. (A) This is expressed by the sentence: "Our laborious Manner of Life compar'd with theirs, they esteem slavish & base."

161. (D) Speaking well (A), hunting and fighting (B), and running (C) are all mentioned in the passage as something that was important for the young Indian men to learn to do. Smoking meats, however, would have fallen under the category of women's work: "The Indian Women till the Ground, dress the Food [etc.]."

162. (A) In the last paragraph, the Indian chiefs turn down the offer to send their young men to college because they considered the other young men that had gone there to be worthless when they returned.

163. (A) The first passage is autobiographical. The author relates a time he remembers fondly from childhood. In the second passage, Benjamin Franklin uses some irony when he shows that civility is a matter of perspective. Choices (B), (C), and (D) can't be right because Passage 1 is very personal and it is not humorous or objective.

164. (C) In Passage 1 the author compares his grandmother to a muskrat. He also called the sap in the trees their lifeblood. Choice (A) is incorrect because the author does not use hyperbole. Choice (B) is incorrect because both authors use examples. Choice (D) does not work because no significant alliteration is used.

165. (C) Choice (A) is not right because the author portrays the Indian life as very busy. The author doesn't comment on the talkativeness of Indians (B), and although (D) is true, this has no bearing on the passage. Choice (C) is the most logical because Passage 1 portrays a grandmother working busily.

166. (C) The best answer is hardworking compared to relaxed. The first passage says: "My grandmother worked like a beaver in these days." The second passage says: "they have abundance of Leisure for Improvement by Conversation." Choice (A) isn't correct because Passage 1 is no simpler than Passage 2. Choice (B) can't be right because the first passage had structure also. Choice (D) is also wrong because although the second passage goes into more detail than the first, there is no reason to think that one is more advanced than the other.

167. (A) Answer choice (A) is the only answer choice that fits the context of the second paragraph.

168. (C) Like all electromagnetic particles, light travels in waves. Only blue light has a wavelength of 450 to 500 nanometers, so answer choice (A) is incorrect.

169. (C) The main point isn't that LED screens emit blue light (answer choice (A)) or that the research was conducted in a controlled setting (answer choice (B)).

170. (B) *Cognitive* most nearly means "mental" and includes the areas of perception, memory, and reasoning, and *performance* means "process."

171. (A) The huge increase in the use of tablets, e-readers, and smartphones causes concern, because they are held closer to the eyes, with increased exposure to blue-light emissions.

172. (B) The entire paragraph is about melatonin, and the key point is that the hormone regulates our daily sleep/wake cycle. The other answer choices are merely supporting details.

173. (D) The National Sleep Foundation is cited as the source for answer choice (A), so this answer choice is incorrect. While answer choices (B) and (C) are mentioned in the passage, neither is associated with the two research projects.

174. (C) Wearing a dimesimeter, a recording device, would not accomplish anything. Watching movies on TV (answer choice (A)), cutting down on nighttime use of the computer (answer choice (B)), and using f.lux (answer choice (D)) are all ways to reduce the melatonin-lowering effects of blue light.

175. (D) The author cites data from the National Sleep Foundation to make readers aware of the possible consequences of excessive nighttime computer use. Melatonin supplements (answer choice (A)) aren't discussed in the passage, and nowhere does the passage suggest that replacing fluorescent lighting (answer choice (C)) would help readers get more sleep.

176. (C) The first lines of the paragraph state that the RPI findings "built on what the Basel researchers discovered."

177. (D) The author hopes that f.lux software is only the first step in finding ways to control blue light.

178. (A) While blue light's rays are shorter than those of visible light, they aren't the shortest. The other answer choices accurately describe blue light.

179. (B) It is logical to assume that the RPI engineers feel that their study offers useful information to computer users, especially those who often use the computer at night.

180. (A) The other answer choices are found in the passage, but they are details—not the main idea.

181. (C) This deduction is based on information in the early part of the passage. Answer choice (B) might be correct, but there isn't any evidence to support it. Based on what the author tells the reader about Theodoric, answer choice (D) is incorrect.

182. (C) Theodoric didn't realize that his traveling companion was blind until the end of the passage. Although answer choice (D) is appealing, most people don't do odd things when they travel.

183. (A) While all of the events were important, the disclosure affects the outcome of the story the most.

184. (D) The other answer choices aren't indicated by the information in the passage.

185. (C) This is the reason that Theodoric decided to put his clothes back on; the train was approaching the station and he would be seen by many people.

186. (D) The mouse's crawling in his pants and biting him forced Theodoric to do something he would never have done otherwise.

187. (D) The author uses a somewhat figurative way to express that the mouse was inside Theodoric's clothes. There is no suggestion that the mouse was nesting in Theodoric's clothes, so answer choice (A) is incorrect.

188. (B) Theodoric is embarrassed and wants to give a logical reason why he has the rug over himself. Theodoric doesn't suggest that it is cold on the train, so answer choice (A) is incorrect.

189. (A) It is clear from the way in which the author writes about Theodoric that he finds him humorous.

190. (B) Theodoric is worried that his traveling companion will be horrified that he doesn't have all his clothes on and will call for help.

191. (B) Theodoric thinks that the traveling companion is having a good time at his expense.

192. (C) The author knows that the traveling companion's blindness is a very important detail, so answer choice (A) is incorrect. (B) and (D) are not supported by the text.

193. (C) The author obviously has fun writing the story and uses a tongue-in-cheek tone.

194. (B) Theodoric was surprised and perhaps somewhat angry, but he most certainly was relieved that his companion had not seen him with his clothes off.

Chapter 4: Set 4 Reading Questions

195. (B) The narrator sees that he will never study French again and that Monsieur Hamel will be leaving; his life will never be the same.

196. (D) Frantz wanted to skip school, but he did not. Nothing in the passage suggests that he wanted to help his teacher (answer choice (A)) or that he wanted to speak to the Prussians (answer choice (C)).

197. (A) The villagers came to show respect to the teacher and say goodbye to him. The Prussians, not the villagers, decided that the teacher should be let go, so answer choice (B) is incorrect.

198. (C) This is an example of foreshadowing. Frantz understood that something was not right because of how solemn the class was.

199. (B) There is no indication of a tradition of the villagers' presence when Frantz was in trouble, so answer choice (A) is incorrect. There is no evidence that the villagers' presence caused Frantz to become even more nervous (answer choice (C)) or to forget his lesson (answer choice (D)).

200. (B) Monsieur Hamel showed greater patience with Frantz than before, when he punished him with his ruler.

201. (C) Frantz was extremely upset that Monsieur Hamel would be gone.

202. (C) This is the main point of the passage and the lesson that it teaches.

203. (C) Monsieur Hamel realizes that Frantz has lost his chance to study French and that Frantz feels badly.

204. (B) The lesson was not easier, so answer choice (A) is incorrect. Frantz was not less concerned about doing well, so answer choice (C) is incorrect. There is no indication that it was a repeated lesson, so answer choice (D) is incorrect.

205. (D) The use of *blared* tells the reader that the author didn't look favorably on the Prussians.

206. (B) Monsieur Hamel's attitude might have been even stronger: he may have hated the Prussians.

207. (D) The fact that he must leave after teaching and living in the building for 40 years was like a death to him.

208. (D) Since Monsieur Hamel wrote his message on the board, it is unlikely that he forgot what he needed to say (answer choice (A)) or didn't know what to say (answer choice (B)). There is no indication that he was losing his voice (answer choice (C)).

209. (A) This is the most likely reason that they turned back.

210. (B) A close reading of the passage makes it clear that the Venetians thought his book was all lies.

211. (B) Nothing in the passage suggests that the princess did not enjoy traveling by herself (answer choice (A)), that she was hesitant to leave her homeland (answer choice (C)), or that she might run away (answer choice (D)).

212. (C) The paragraph identifies the failure to mention the Great Wall of China as one of the historians' reasons.

213. (A) This is probably the best proof; there is a saying that dying men tell no lies.

214. (C) Ericson's Viking history is only mentioned in relation to his seafaring and exploring tendencies. Although we know from other sources that the Vikings were violent (A), that is not detailed in this passage. Neither pride of heritage (B) nor a comparison of civilizations (D) is supported by the passage either.

215. (D) There are a few context clues that support this choice. He was *disappointed* in Baffin Island because it was barren and rocky. He was *rewarded* by his travels when he found salmon, green pastures, and timberland. Although the passage indicates he was interested in converting Greenland to Christianity, there is no mention of his looking for converts on his travels to North America (B). There is no support for (A) or (C) in the passage either.

216. (B) There are many indications that Ericson liked to travel, including his first trip to Norway as well as his trip west. None of the other options are discussed in the passage.

217. (A) Before the find, all of the information about Leif Ericson sailing to North America was based on legend. Tourism was never mentioned (B), and the passage does not indicate that Ericson is as famous as Columbus (D). The find probably did help historians to better understand Viking culture (C), but that is not indicated by the passage.

218. (B) Other stories about Vikings may have told us that they were cruel and ruthless (A), but this passage does not indicate that. The only land settlement the paragraph mentions is Greenland—that is not *many* (C). The history of the Vikings is not mentioned in the paragraph (D).

219. (B) Passage 1 has a direct quote of Marco Polo's. Passage 2 does not quote Leif Ericson. Both passages follow a chronological timeline (A), neither is argumentative (C), and only Passage 2 references archaeologists' data.

220. (B) Both passages focus on relating the adventures and discoveries of explorers. In Passage 1, over time, people come to realize that Marco Polo was telling the truth, and in Passage 2, the discovery of the Viking settlement in Newfoundland changed the history of North America (A), but neither of these points was central to the passages. Both passages mention spreading Christianity (C), but neither focuses on that point. Marco Polo's book did change Europe's perception of the world (D), but that point is not really made in Passage 2.

221. (A) Passage 2 is about a discovery changing what we knew about history. Although the discovery in Passage 2 did confirm stories that had been passed down for generations (C), there is not enough evidence in the text to suggest the author felt that stories should never be challenged. There is no evidence about how the author felt about a consensus (B) or about what should be taught in schools (D).

222. (C) In Passage 1, Marco Polo's stories are disregarded and later proven to be true. In Passage 2, Viking legends are proven to be based on fact with the discovery of L'Anse aux Meadows. Although sea travel is dangerous in Passage 1 (A), there is no comment on its dangers or lack thereof in Passage 2. Passage 1 does not imply only proven historical facts should be trusted (B), and neither passage indicates that the explorations took place in order to expand Christianity (D).

223. (C) The author says that in winter "the moon achieves a fuller triumph," that is, it seems bigger.

224. (B) Winter brings out the sinewy part of the mind, not imagination (answer choice (A)), passion (answer choice (C)), or sadness (answer choice (D)).

225. (A) Answer choice (A) describes winter, not summer.

226. (A) According to the author, winter is a time for "studies and disciplines."

227. (C) There is no mention in the paragraph that winter is a victim of summer (answer choice (A)), that it gives less joy than summer (answer choice (B)), or that it is harder to live through (answer choice (D)).

228. (C) The author is romantic, but sees deeply into things. There is no suggestion that the author is overwrought and tense, so answer choice (A) is incorrect. The author might be considered intellectual, but he is hardly pragmatic, so answer choice (B) is incorrect. There is no suggestion that the author is cynical and despairing (answer choice (D))—quite the opposite.

229. (B) The paragraph does state that snow makes the fence look like iron (answer choice (A)), but that is a detail—not the main idea.

230. (B) The work that the chopper does warms his body. He may be wearing a heavy sweater (answer choice (A)), but that isn't the point that the author is making.

231. (A) The first sentence of the paragraph states, "All sounds are sharper in winter; the air transmits better" (line 43). This is reinforced in the next sentence, which states that another sound is heard "more distinctly."

232. (D) The author makes it clear that he isn't talking about conventional heat. There is no mention of making a fire more easily (answer choice (A)) or the air being dry (answer choice (B)).

233. (D) The author enjoys the sound of the fox and imagines things about the animal. It doesn't annoy (answer choice (A)) or frighten (answer choice (B)) him. Nor does he find it chilling (answer choice (C)).

234. (B) The author likens winter to an artist several times in the passage.

235. (C) Winter isn't sentimental; summer is.

236. (D) The snow keeps a record of the footprints of animals and people.

237. (A) Gravity is a consequence of distortion in space and time, according to Einstein. The other answer choices are all characteristics of black holes.

238. (D) The passage states that Einstein foreshadowed the possibility of the existence of black holes in 1915.

239. (C) NuSTAR measures high-energy X-ray light (lines 41–42).

240. (B) By measuring the speed and orbit of stars and interstellar gases as they orbit a black hole, scientists can measure the mass of the black hole.

241. (C) The Chandra X-ray Observatory can measure X-rays that are absorbed by the atmosphere and cannot be detected on Earth. The phrase "read a stop sign from a distance of 12 miles" (answer choice (A)) is used by the author merely to indicate the acuity of the telescope.

242. (C) By quoting from the autobiography of Dr. Wheeler at the end of the passage, the author makes clear that the nature of the universe may never be fully understood.

243. (A) When the star collapses on itself, its mass becomes infinitely dense and is known as a singularity.

244. (A) The paragraph states this statistic as 24 million miles vs. 93 million miles, or slightly more than 25%. Sgr A* has a mass equivalent to 4 million suns, so answer choice (C) is incorrect. Answer choices (B) and (D) are facts, not inferences.

245. (B) Newton defined gravity as a force, a theory that was superseded by Einstein's *General Theory of Relativity*.

246. (C) The first sentence of the ninth paragraph states that "some people believe that black holes are 'wormholes' that lead to another dimension and another universe." Answer choices (A) and (B) are false statements. Wormholes might be a fantasy (answer choice (D)), but there is no way to prove the theory.

247. (D) Although his autobiography is quoted in the last paragraph, Dr. Wheeler is best known for first using the term "black hole."

248. (D) Because nothing can enter a black hole without being destroyed, there is no way to prove any theory about whether black holes lead anywhere.

249. (C) According to the passage, "the gravitational attraction nearly equals the speed of light" at the event horizon (lines 24–25), so you would be overwhelmed.

250. (C) Dr. Wheeler is saying that these laws aren't permanent.

Chapter 5: Set 1 English Questions

251. (A) No comma or semicolon is required between *Party* and *and*, because *and* joins two parallel phrases and doesn't require any punctuation; nor is there a need for a comma after *and*.

252. (D) No transition word is required here, because the sentence introduces information about Alice Paul that isn't directly linked to the preceding sentence.

253. (D) A serial comma is required before *and*, because this is a series of degrees that Paul received.

254. (B) Since the action took place in the past, the verb should reflect that. The verb form *having traveled* creates a phrase rather than a sentence; a sentence is required.

255. (A) This simple past verb form is correct. Answer choices (B) and (C) change the sentence to a phrase.

256. (D) No transition word is required here.

257. (D) The transition word *while* makes the most sense, since it links the time of Paul's being in prison to what she was doing.

258. (D) Including the name that the press gave the demonstrations shows that the press was characterizing them.

259. (B) The word *but* shows the correct relationship between the two parts of the sentence.

260. (B) Since the action took place in the past, the verb should reflect that. Answer choice (A) is incorrect, because this verb form creates a phrase rather than a sentence. Answer choice (C) is an incorrect past tense, since it shows an ongoing action. Answer choice (D) is also an incorrect past tense.

261. (B) This verb form introduces a phrase that modifies *banners*.

262. (D) The verb forms *denied* and *abridged* are part of the sentence and should not be set off by commas.

263. (A) This is the correct past-tense verb form. Answer choice (B) is incorrect, because an amendment cannot *ratify*; it can only *be ratified*. Answer choices (C) and (D) are incorrect verb forms; they are in the present tense.

264. (B) This is where the sentence logically belongs. It is too important a detail to omit, so answer choice (D) is incorrect.

265. (C) The action takes place in the past, so a past-tense verb form is required.

266. (C) The conjunction *still* creates the correct relationship between the two parts of the sentence.

267. (D) This is the most concise way to express the idea. The other answer choices are awkward and wordy.

268. (D) There is no need for the words *they were*; all that needs to follow the colon is the names of the explorers.

269. (A) The word *exposure* succinctly incorporates the concepts of very cold weather and lack of warm clothing.

270. (D) This is the most concise and exact way to communicate how high the station is above sea level.

271. (B) This is the strongest description of the weather at the South Pole; it gives the reader a sense of danger by using the words *severe* and *life-threatening*.

272. (D) Answer choice (D) isn't acceptable as an alternative to *Consequently*. All of the other answer choices could be substituted for *Consequently*.

273. (B) *Swells* is much more precise and descriptive than the other answer choices of what happens to the population of scientists.

274. (C) By eliminating these two words, the reader would lose the sense of a contrast between where the station is located and how many scientists work there.

275. (C) This gives more specific information about the scientific disciplines that make use of the research station.

276. (C) This is the most succinct and direct way to include information about light pollution. The other answer choices are wordy or convoluted.

277. (D) This information is of minor importance to the main topic of the paragraph.

278. (B) A comma is necessary after this opening phrase. Answer choices (C) and (D) would make the opening phrase an incomplete sentence.

279. (B) This is the most succinct and direct way to link the series. The other answer choices include unnecessary and repetitive adverbs.

280. (D) The word *However* should be omitted, since there is no relationship between this sentence and the preceding one. Answer choice (B) is incorrect, since the word *Because* would make the sentence incomplete.

281. (B) This word agrees in number with the subject of the sentence, *scientists*. Answer choice (D) is incorrect, because it would leave the sentence without a verb.

282. (D) There is no basis for the other three answer choices.

283. (C) This is the most succinct way to express this idea. Answer choices (A) and (B) are overly wordy and awkward. The sentence wouldn't make sense if the preposition were removed, so answer choice (D) is incorrect.

284. (A) A comma is required after the opening phrase, which describes El Yunque. Answer choices (C) and (D) would make the opening phrase an incomplete sentence.

285. (C) This provides the strongest and most precise description of the views. Answer choice (A) is rather vague. Answer choice (B) would be ungrammatical. Answer choice (D) would leave the views without a description.

286. (D) This provides a vivid image of the clouds. The other answer choices are imprecise and weak descriptors.

287. (C) The sentence only makes sense using this word sequence.

288. (D) This is a possessive form. Answer choice (B) is incorrect for two reasons: lack of a possessive form and omission of the necessary comma. There is only one mountain, so answer choice (C) is incorrect.

289. (A) This is the most succinct and direct way of communicating this information. The other answer choices are unwieldy and awkward.

290. (B) This language is strong and provides a vivid image, making the writing much more interesting and colorful. Answer choices (A) and (C) are vague and uninteresting. Answer choice (D) would result in an incomplete phrase.

291. (A) This word alerts the reader to information that is amazing. Answer choice (B) is incorrect, since it implies a negative relationship with the preceding sentence. Answer choice (C) is contrary to the meaning of the sentence. Answer choice (D) would leave out an important clue about the large number of tree varieties found in El Yunque.

292. (D) Without the word *exotic*, the reader would not realize that these varieties of vegetation are unusual.

293. (B) This provides important information about the trails. The other answer choices add little or no new information.

294. (B) This sentence needs a subject and a verb, and the contraction *it's*, for *it is*, provides these. Answer choice (A) is a possessive form, not a contraction. Answer choice (C) is grammatically incorrect. Answer choice (D) would result in an incomplete sentence.

295. (D) This placement is the most logical and helps the reader understand what the bird looks like. The other answer choices render the sentence extremely confusing or ungrammatical.

296. (A) This fits the notion of the coquí calling out during the evening hours. Answer choice (B) is mundane. Answer choices (C) and (D) would apply to a person, not an animal.

297. (C) The idea expressed in Sentence 5 naturally follows the idea expressed in Sentence 3.

298. (C) The use of *you* would personalize the sense that the writer wants to convey. The other answer choices are not accurate.

299. (B) The phrase describing Timbuktu, "a famous city in western Africa," should be set off by commas.

300. (D) Since these clauses contain two distinct thoughts, each one should be its own sentence.

301. (C) This is the most effective closing sentence; it sums up the information in the preceding sentences. The other answer choices provide details, but not a summary.

302. (B) The simple past verb form fits the context here.

303. (B) A possessive form is required to show that this represents a time (period) of six months. Since "six months" is plural, the singular possessive in answer choice (C) is incorrect.

304. (B) This tells of Cox and Abdul becoming friends—important information for understanding the rest of the essay.

305. (B) The simple past verb form fits the context here.

306. (B) The past participle *taken* matches *sold*. The simple past form *was* fits the context.

307. (B) The pronoun *who* refers to a person (in this case, Abdul); *that* and *which* are used with objects, so answer choices (A) and (D) are incorrect. *Whom* isn't used when the pronoun is the subject of its clause, so answer choice (C) is incorrect.

308. (D) This sequence shows that 17 years passed between Abdul's enslavement and Cox's discovery of him in Mississippi.

309. (B) The superlative form of the adjective makes the most sense. *Mostest* isn't grammatical, so answer choice (C) is incorrect.

310. (A) The simple infinitive form is correct in this construction with *sent*.

311. (B) The phrase is evidence that the writer researched the subject.

312. (D) The phrase "through diplomacy" modifies "developing trade and good relations" and should be placed with it.

313. (A) Although answer choice (B) expresses the same thought as answer choice (A), it isn't as well written. The other answer choices are convoluted.

314. (B) A comma is required after the conjunctive adverb *however*.

315. (C) Since these clauses contain two distinct ideas, each one should be its own sentence and they should be separated by a period.

316. (D) The tense of the verb in the subordinate clause should agree with the tense of the main verb (the present tense).

317. (D) The past participle *affected* needs a verb to make this a complete sentence; *can be* makes the most sense.

318. (A) The underlined portion is correctly punctuated.

319. (B) The word *terror* most effectively indicates the intense fear that a tsunami evokes.

320. (C) The colon introduces an explanation of what a tsunami is.

321. (D) The antecedent is "tidal waves," so the pronoun should be *they*. Since the verb in the main clause is in the present tense, the verb in this clause should also be in the present tense.

322. (D) Although this information doesn't contradict earlier statements, it doesn't advance the main idea of the essay; it distracts the reader.

323. (B) This phrase modifies *called* and should be placed immediately before it.

324. (C) The infinitive is required in the construction with *causes*.

325. (A) The conjunctive adverb *however* introduces a new and complete idea and therefore needs to be part of a separate sentence.

326. (B) Use of the comparative form of *shallow* is correct, since only two items are being compared: the depth of the ocean farther and closer to shore.

327. (D) The present participle matches the earlier verb form *pulling*.

328. (D) Since the subject ("The Pacific Tsunami Warning Center") is singular, the verb must be singular. The tense of the verb should be the same as that of the earlier verb, *monitors*, that is, present tense.

329. (A) *It's* is the contracted form of *it has*, which is grammatically correct. The other answer choices are ungrammatical.

330. (D) Paragraph 2 logically introduces the essay and therefore should be placed first.

331. (B) Since "noted thinker" and "Joseph Campbell" are in apposition, there should be no comma after *thinker*.

332. (A) The writer is letting the reader know what he thinks of the advice that follows.

333. (D) A superlative comparison is being made, so answer choice (B) is incorrect. Answer choices (A) and (C) are ungrammatical.

334. (B) This is where the phrase logically belongs. The other answer choices make the sentence confusing and illogical.

335. (B) *Stressful* is a strong descriptor. The other answer choices are weak and vague.

336. (D) The word *to* is incorrect in this construction. Since the tense of the verb should match that of the main clause, answer choices (B) and (C) are incorrect.

337. (C) The original construction is a run-on sentence and needs to be made into two sentences by inserting a period and capitalizing the first word of the second sentence.

338. (D) Since the items in this serial list are separated by commas, there should be a comma after *artistic*.

339. (D) The word *as* is incorrect, because *machine* and *computer* both modify *repairman*.

340. (A) This is valuable information about conventional people and why they choose the jobs they do, so it should be included.

341. (D) This is a serial list of the kinds of jobs that conventional personality types do, so there needs to be a comma between the job possibilities *clerical work* and *accounting*.

342. (A) The transition word *However* contrasts the information in the preceding sentence with the information in its sentence.

343. (D) *As well as* introduces an incomplete sentence and needs to be joined to the preceding sentence.

344. (A) This is where Sentence 1 logically belongs.

345. (C) The article doesn't discuss various career aspects; it discusses personality types and which careers are most suitable for certain personalities.

346. (A) A possessive form is required to show that this represents a trip of one day. Since "a day" is singular, the plural possessive in answer choice (C) is incorrect.

347. (A) This is the clearest and most succinct way to express this fact. Answer choice (D) is incorrect, because it would delete important information.

348. (D) The phrases in answer choices (A), (B), and (C) are unnecessary and cumbersome.

349. (D) This adds significant information to the essay. The other answer choices are vague.

350. (D) The word *nostalgic* tells the reader that the writer was feeling wistful about the past.

351. (B) The original construction is a run-on sentence and needs to be made into two sentences by inserting a period and capitalizing the first word of the second sentence.

352. (D) The past perfect tense (with the correct past participle, *chosen*) is correct.

353. (D) This provides concise and important information. Answer choice (B) is incorrect, since children are people.

354. (B) This clause is direct and concise. Answer choice (A) is slightly awkward, and answer choice (C) is wordy. Answer choice (D) is ungrammatical.

355. (A) This descriptive word gives the reader an idea of what the town was like.

356. (D) This is where the phrase logically belongs, since it tells what the women were doing with the pots.

357. (D) The word *However* suggests a contrasting relationship between this sentence and the preceding one, but none exists, so it should be deleted.

358. (B) A comma is required between two clauses that are connected by a transition word.

359. (B) Paragraph 2 logically introduces the essay and therefore should be placed first.

360. (A) The writer contrasts his memories of Sherbro Island with his feelings as he revisits it.

361. (C) *It's* is the contracted form of *it is*, which is grammatically correct. *Its'* is ungrammatical, so answer choice (B) is incorrect. *They're* (answer choice (D)) is plural and makes no sense in this context.

362. (B) The original construction is a run-on sentence and needs to be made into two sentences by inserting a period and capitalizing the first word of the second sentence.

363. (D) The conditional verb *would* is correct after *knew*.

364. (B) The simple past verb form *liked* matches the simple past form *grew* earlier in the sentence. Answer choice (C) is ungrammatical, and answer choice (D) is awkward.

365. (D) The clause is logically placed at the end of the sentence.

366. (A) The other answer choices add little detail.

367. (C) There is no reason to suppose that the writer cleaned only the *dirtier* or *dirtiest* cages, so answer choices (A) and (D) are incorrect. Answer choice (B) isn't grammatical.

368. (C) The relative pronoun *who* refers to people, while *that* refers to animals and objects; therefore, answer choices (A) and (B) are incorrect. Since the pronoun is necessary, answer choice (D) is incorrect.

369. (D) This information is included earlier in the sentence.

370. (B) The tense of the verb in the subordinate clause must match that of the main verb (the simple past tense).

371. (B) The original construction is a run-on sentence and needs to be made into two sentences by inserting a period. Answer choice (C) also creates a run-on sentence.

372. (B) *Consequently* doesn't make sense in this context. The other answer choices have the approximate meaning of *however.*

373. (D) The singular possessive of *year* is required here.

374. (A) The simple past tense matches the tense of *sent* later in the sentence.

375. (B) This is where Sentence 2, as an introductory sentence, logically belongs.

Chapter 6: Set 2 English Questions

376. (B) A comma is required after the name of the state.

377. (D) The word *However* suggests a contrasting relationship between this sentence and the preceding one, but none exists, so it should be deleted.

378. (B) The inclusion of the fact that women were rare in early aviation shows how special Amelia Earhart was.

379. (D) Since the decision took place in the past, the verb should be in the simple past tense.

380. (B) This is the most concise way to provide the information. Answer choice (A) doesn't modify any element in the rest of the sentence. Answer choices (C) and (D) are wordy.

381. (A) The word *with* completes the meaning of the verb *outfitted*. Answer choices (B) and (C) would create an ungrammatical sentence. Answer choice (D) is incorrect, because it would eliminate important information.

382. (A) A comma is required between the opening phrase, which modifies *she*, and the main clause. Answer choice (D) would create an incomplete sentence before the period.

383. (C) The simple past tense is the correct form of the verb. Answer choice (A) is incorrect, since Noonan was not in the act of charting.

384. (D) Since the antecedent of this word is *they*, the plural possessive form is required.

385. (C) *Where* is required, because the clause that follows concerns the location of the airfield and fuel tanks. The other answer choices are ungrammatical.

386. (B) This is the only answer choice of transition words that cannot be substituted for *though*.

387. (C) This is where Sentence 6 logically belongs. Answer choice (D) is incorrect, because it would delete important information.

388. (D) This is where the phrase logically belongs. The other answer choices are awkward or confusing.

389. (B) A conjunction is required to connect *to send* and *(to) see*.

390. (D) The simple past tense form of the verb is required.

391. (C) This statement about Noonan's career is an unimportant detail in an essay about the ill-fated flight of Earhart and Noonan.

392. (B) This placement makes the most sense. The other answer choices are awkward or change the meaning of the sentence.

393. (C) This is the simplest and most straightforward way of stating the information. The other answer choices are ungrammatical or contain redundant words.

394. (A) The other answer choices change the meaning of the sentence.

395. (B) Elimination of *exotic* and "from the East" would remove the idea that the items were not easily obtained because they came from far away.

396. (D) A comma is required after the opening adverb. Since *merchants* is the subject of the sentence, the possessive form is not used.

397. (A) A comma is required after the opening phrase. Answer choices (C) and (D) would create an incomplete sentence.

398. (B) This transition word correctly shows a cause-and-effect relationship between the preceding sentence and this sentence. Answer choices (A) and (C) incorrectly suggest a contrasting relationship. Answer choice (D) incorrectly suggests that there is no relationship between the two sentences.

399. (B) The sentence contains two distinct ideas and should be separated into two sentences.

400. (B) The actual figures spent on television advertising provide a sense of the huge amount of money involved.

401. (D) Since the subject (*advertising*) is singular, the verb must be singular. Answer choice (B) is plural, so it is incorrect. Answer choices (A) and (C) are ungrammatical.

402. (A) This important information would be lost.

403. (D) A superlative form of the adverb is required, since there is a range of probabilities, not just two. Answer choice (B) is ungrammatical. Answer choice (C) is a comparative adjective.

404. (C) This information is unnecessary and distracts from the main focus of the paragraph.

405. (C) This reads smoothly. Answer choice (A) is awkward, and answer choice (B) is ungrammatical. Answer choice (D) would eliminate the word that links the location of this sentence with that of the preceding one.

406. (D) This is where the paragraph belongs in terms of sequence and logic. The other answer choices wouldn't make sense.

407. (A) The writer has successfully fulfilled his goal by demonstrating the significance of advertising through the years.

408. (B) A comma is required after *Nakota* to separate the serial list from the phrase beginning with *comprising*.

409. (D) This is the clearest and most direct of the answer choices. Answer choice (B) is ungrammatical.

410. (D) This phrase provides the most significant information.

411. (C) This is a serial list of gerunds, so there needs to be a comma between the second and third gerund phrases, "gathering foodstuffs" and "caring for their young." Answer choice (B) would create an incomplete sentence.

412. (D) The preposition *with* is required to show the relationship between "nature" and "the animals they hunted."

413. (B) The action has occurred for generations up to the present, and the verb form must be in the passive voice.

414. (A) The story of the rainbow happened in the past, and *to be* correctly follows *came* in this idiom.

415. (B) The adverb *consequently*, formed by adding *-ly* to the adjective *consequent*, is correct. *Consequence* is a noun and cannot be converted to an adverb, so answer choice (C) is incorrect. The phrase *with consequence* makes no sense, so answer choice (D) is incorrect.

416. (B) The adjective *integral*, meaning "essential to completeness," is more precise than answer choices (A) and (C). Answer choice (D) makes no sense.

417. (D) Sentence 5 should be placed after Sentence 7.

418. (D) This phrase is clear and straightforward. The other answer choices are awkward or ungrammatical.

419. (B) *Culminating* means "coming to a climax or ending" and describes *series*. *Concomitant* and *cascading* don't make sense in this context. The adverb *collaterally* would make the sentence ungrammatical.

420. (A) Sitting Bull was chief of the Sioux. The other answer choices obscure or contradict this fact.

421. (C) *The Sioux* is a collective plural, and the verb must be in the present tense because the reference is to *today.* Answer choice (D) is awkward.

422. (A) The phrase "their native" is specific and clear.

423. (A) The statement explains why the site is revered and sacred.

424. (C) The progressive tense is used to express an ongoing action when another action took place.

425. (D) Since these clauses contain two distinct thoughts, each one should be its own sentence.

426. (B) The word *excitedly* adds the nuance that the writer was thrilled by the discovery of the turtles.

427. (A) The simple past tense is required to match the tense of *looked up* and *belonged,* so answer choices (B) and (C) are incorrect. Answer choice (D) is incorrect, because a comma is required to separate the initial adverbial phrase from the rest of the sentence.

428. (C) *Inhabits,* which means "lives in," makes the most sense here.

429. (C) *Must have been* is the only answer choice that is grammatical.

430. (A) The phrase should be placed where it is now, because the phrase "to support them" must immediately follow "an aquatic environment," which it modifies.

431. (B) *Would* is required in a clause that begins "on the condition that."

432. (C) The simple past tense *started* matches the tense of *seemed.*

433. (A) This additional information is important, because it helps the reader understand why the writer fed the turtles lettuce.

434. (C) *Lying* is the gerund of the verb *to lie,* which means "to be in a reclining position." *Laying* means "putting down," so answer choice (A) is incorrect. *Lain* is the past participle of *lie,* so answer choice (B) is incorrect. *To lay* means "to put down," so answer choice (D) is incorrect.

435. (C) It is best to divide the awkward sentence into two separate sentences; this makes the meaning clearer.

436. (B) *Would become* is the correct verb form; it shows the writer's speculation based on the preceding sentence.

437. (A) This answer choice reveals the writer's feelings most effectively. Answer choices (B) and (C) are vague, and answer choice (D) is inaccurate.

438. (A) Paragraph 1 sets the stage for the essay, and Paragraph 2 provides more details about the turtles. Paragraph 4 relates events that occurred after the events of Paragraph 3.

439. (B) The essay tells of the writer's acceptance of change and fulfills the goal of illustrating that life is full of unexpected turns.

440. (C) The preposition *throughout* is most appropriate and makes the meaning clearest. The other answer choices are awkward or misleading.

441. (B) The tense of the verb in the subordinate clause must match the simple past tense of the verb in the main clause, *was.*

442. (A) *Imaginative* suggests that the two teenagers were talented.

443. (A) This answer choice best substantiates the claims about Superman's powers. The other answer choices are vague.

444. (A) This answer choice adds an important description of Superman's powers. The other answer choices are awkward or less specific.

445. (B) *Could*, which indicates possibility, matches *could* in the preceding sentence.

446. (D) No transition word is required, since the sentence is unrelated to the preceding sentence.

447. (D) As his alter ego, Superman purposefully chose to be *mild-mannered.*

448. (B) This is the most direct expression; it reads more clearly than answer choice (A). Answer choices (C) and (D) would make the sentence ungrammatical.

449. (B) The phrase "as if" makes the most sense after *feel.*

450. (D) *Helpless* is the most appropriate word in this context. *Prostrate* means "lying face down," *servile* means "submissive," and *rejected* means "spurned" or "abandoned."

451. (C) The statement would distract the reader without adding any important information.

452. (A) The transition word *besides* makes no sense. Answer choices (B), (C), and (D) mean about the same as *but.*

453. (A) *Think the reason is* makes sense and is grammatically correct; the other answer choices are ungrammatical.

454. (C) *Truly*, which means "really" or "doubtlessly," best completes the sentence. *Seemingly* and *apparently* imply doubt, so answer choices (A) and (B) are incorrect. Omission of *seemingly* would weaken the notion that Superman cares about people.

455. (B) The quotation marks add authenticity to Superman's mission in life.

456. (C) The superlative form of the adjective is required for clarity, and *one of* requires the plural *women*. Answer choice (D) would result in a nonsensical sentence.

457. (D) This answer choice provides specific, relevant information.

458. (C) It is logical that she took the name afterwards. Answer choices (A) and (D) are ungrammatical.

459. (B) No comma is used before a restrictive clause. The use of *under* changes the meaning of the sentence, so answer choice (D) is incorrect.

460. (D) The underlined phrase should be eliminated. *Plethora* means "excess," which is clearly not the writer's intention. Answer choice (B) means about the same thing, while answer choice (C) means the opposite.

461. (A) Since the preceding verbs are in the simple past tense, it would be awkward to use another tense here.

462. (C) The passive voice requires the past particle *invited.* Answer choice (B) is ungrammatical. *Oft*, while sometimes acceptable in poetry, is archaic and inappropriate in this essay, so answer choice (D) is incorrect.

463. (B) The possessive plural, *women's*, must be used before *rights.*

464. (D) Answer choices (A) and (B) are ungrammatical. Since the relative pronoun *that* is used with animals and things, but not with people, answer choice (C) is incorrect. In this construction, *whom* may be understood.

465. (A) When a question mark is part of a title that is followed by a comma, the comma is placed after the closing quotation mark, so answer choice (C) is incorrect. Answer choice (B) is incorrect, because the question mark is part of the title of the speech and must be placed inside the closing quotation mark. Since the title must be set off by commas before and after, answer choice (D) is incorrect.

466. (D) The antecedent is *injustice*, so the singular pronoun *it* is used.

467. (C) The other answer choices are ungrammatical.

468. (A) The other answer choices are awkward and ungrammatical.

469. (C) Sentence 10 explains the purpose of the Freedmen's Bureau, which is mentioned in Sentence 3.

470. (D) The infinitive of *retire* is required in the construction with *caused*. The other answer choices are ungrammatical.

471. (A) *Let us* has a very formal tone in this context; changing *us* to *me* would make the tone less formal and more personal.

472. (D) The preposition *while* establishes the proper relationship between *duties* and *rewards*.

473. (D) No transition phrase is required, since the ideas in the preceding sentence and this one aren't connected. Answer choice (C) makes no sense.

474. (B) The survey took place in the past, so the simple past tense is required. The passive voice in answer choice (D) would create an ungrammatical sentence.

475. (A) No punctuation is necessary. Answer choice (B) creates an incomplete sentence.

476. (D) The past progressive tense is used to match *were finishing* earlier in the sentence.

477. (C) The conjunction *after* makes the most sense in this context, because he continued smiling after he took his uniform. *Taking* in answer choices (B) and (D) don't match the tense of the verb *gave*.

478. (B) The phrase "in ages" is much stronger than "in a long time."

479. (D) This placement makes the most sense. Answer choice (A) makes it appear that the friends are talking to the mother. Answer choices (B) and (C) are awkward.

480. (A) *Fruition*, which means "achievement" or "fulfillment," is appropriate here. The other words don't make sense.

481. (B) The other answer choices are ungrammatical or nonsensical.

482. (A) Beginning a new sentence with *Plus* highlights the fact that there is even more work to do. Answer choices (C) and (D) would create run-on sentences.

483. (A) *Infinitesimal* means "exceedingly small"—the opposite of *immeasurable*. The other answer choices are close in meaning to *immeasurable*.

484. (C) Paragraph 3 sets the stage for the events of Paragraph 2.

485. (B) The essay clearly demonstrates that life can change quickly due to an emotional experience; in this case, the mother's harried day turned into a day of joy.

486. (D) The sentence is complete and coherent without a conjunction at the beginning; in fact, the conjunction creates an incomplete sentence.

487. (A) "Conquistadors (soldiers of the Spanish Empire)" adds texture and detail to the essay.

488. (C) *Pioneers* is an appositive of the subject *Anglos* and therefore is not possessive, so answer choices (A) and (B) are incorrect. Answer choice (D) incorrectly suggests that all Anglos were English.

489. (D) The tense of *roam* must match the simple past tense of the main verb *came*. The adverbial form *freely* modifies the verb *roamed*.

490. (D) "After the Battle of San Jacinto" is a subordinate clause set off by commas. The other answer choices would create incomplete sentences.

491. (B) *Consequently* correctly links this sentence to the preceding one. Answer choices (A) and (C) establish an incorrect relationship between these sentences. Omitting the linking word reduces the clarity of the paragraph.

492. (C) The simple past tense is used to match *took* earlier in the sentence, so answer choices (B) and (D) are incorrect. *Them* is redundant, so answer choice (A) is incorrect.

493. (A) "These vaqueros" refers to "the vaqueros" in the preceding sentence. *Vaqueros* is plural, so answer choice (B) is incorrect. *Those* in answer choice (C) makes it appear that they are different vaqueros. Answer choice (D) is an incomplete sentence.

494. (D) They wore chaps in order to protect their legs. The other answer choices are ungrammatical.

495. (C) *That* is used to complete the thought introduced by *so many*. The other answer choices are awkward or ungrammatical.

496. (D) The simple past tense is used to match the other verbs in the paragraph, so answer choice (B) is incorrect. The plural *cowboys* must be used to match other uses of the word in the paragraph, so answer choices (A) and (C) are incorrect.

497. (B) Setting *hoosegow* off with dashes is grammatically correct. (It could also be set off with commas.)

498. (C) This answer choice is simple and direct. The other answer choices are awkward or wordy.

499. (B) *Independent* and *self-reliant* are adjectives modifying *cowboy*. No comparison is being made, so using the comparative or superlative forms of these adjectives is incorrect.

500. (C) Sentence 1 is the best opening sentence. The word *also* in Sentence 3 links it to Sentence 1. Sentence 2 is the best closing sentence.